THE QUARTERBACK &
THE BALLERINA

ANNE-MARIE MEYER

MAGGIE DALLEN

The Ballerina Academy

The Ballerina Academy

Copyright © 2020 by Anne-Marie Meyer and Maggie Dallen

All rights reserved.

No part of this book may be reproduced in any form or by any electronic or mechanical means, including information storage and retrieval systems, without written permission from the author, except for the use of brief quotations in a book review.

ONE

ETHAN

When Coach Reynolds told me what he'd planned as punishment for my teammates, I'd thought he was joking. The entire starting lineup for the Oakwood High football team taking ballet lessons? He couldn't be serious.

I stared up at the tall gray building that took up half a block in the nice area of town, my buddies piling out of the cars that had pulled up behind me. *Academie de Ballet* was etched in big, bold letters over the arched entryway at the top of a set of stairs.

Coach had *not* been kidding. I probably should have known he was serious. In the three years I'd been playing for him, the old grouch had never once cracked a joke. Still, I'd thought he'd calm down. I figured he'd come to see reason...

"Dude, the old man has lost it." Cooper Jenkins, our wide receiver, came up to stand beside me. At six feet he was the same height as me, but he was roughly twice the width and that was all muscle. The guy lived and breathed the weight room. Watching Cooper prance around on tiptoe amidst a bunch of petite girls was the one thing that might make this punishment almost seem bearable.

Almost.

"Can't you talk to him?" Cooper said. "The old man loves you."

"Yeah, Ethan," Ryan said from behind me. "You're Coach's favorite little pet. If anyone can make him see reason, it's you." Despite his mockery, Ryan was one of my best friends. He came to stand on my other side, crossing his arms as he too took in the sight of our prison for the next three months.

Until the end of the semester, that's what Coach had said when he'd spelled out our punishment in the locker room.

Cooper turned his glare from the building to me. "Talk to him, Ethan."

"I tried," I said for the millionth time. They'd been pestering me in the halls all day today, seeing if I could get our coach to change his mind. For the record, they came to me because I was the captain, not because I was coach's 'little pet'—whatever that meant.

"Try harder." Cooper's voice was as forbidding as his giant body, but I'd been playing ball with him since middle school so I knew better. Underneath all that muscle, he wasn't all that scary. I mean, he was a *little* scary, but not out of control. If the coach said dance, the big guy would totally dance.

"Come on, dude," Ryan said. "You're the *quarterback*. You've got to have some sway over the old man. Just...threaten to quit the team or something."

Unlike Cooper, Ryan actually *was* something of a wild card. He took nothing seriously, least of all football. Good thing he had mad skills as a running back or he'd have been off the team years ago. As it was, Coach threatened to cut him at least once a week.

"I'm not quitting the team."

"Why not? You don't need the scholarship money." And that right there summed up Ryan's life philosophy to a tee. He didn't understand why anyone would do anything unless there was some sort of financial gain—or a chance to score with girls. Money and girls, that was pretty much all he seemed to care about. And maybe music, I supposed. He did have a band. But again, I was pretty sure playing guitar and forming a band were just another way to get the money and girls.

Music was really the only thing we had in common—we both played guitar. Sometimes we jammed together, and the rest of the time he just tried his best to annoy the crap out of me.

The rest of the guys were out of their cars and starting to gather around me. For a bunch of alpha jocks, none of them seemed eager to lead at this particular moment. Myself included. I eyed the entrance warily. I'd never been to the ballet, I'd never dated a girl who was into ballet, and I sure as heck never danced ballet myself. I had no idea what the coach had gotten us into. He'd been light on the details, just telling us to show up here after practice today.

Everyone was looking to me to lead the way.

"What would he do if we bailed?" That came from Alex, a linebacker. "I mean, it's not like Coach can bench all the starters right?"

I shot Alex a sidelong look that made him squirm. "He can and he would if he thought we were blatantly undermining his authority."

"The guy's a freakin' dictator," Cooper said.

More like a former marine who ran this team like his own personal brigade, but he wasn't too far off base.

"The guy lives to make us miserable," Alex said. "It's like he's just looking for an excuse to ruin our lives."

I turned to face Alex. "Maybe you should have thought of that before you threw a party the night before our first game."

Alex scratched at the back of his head. "It wasn't supposed to be a rager, it just sort of...got out of control."

"Yeah, well, that tends to happen when you invite every person in our school to a house party with no parents and a full keg."

"Okay, Mom," Ryan said, clapping a hand on my shoulder. "What's done is done, right?"

I shrugged him off. "Right." I tried not to be resentful, I really did. But this was not the first time I found myself thinking how unfair it was that I was paying for their mistake. I'd been the only guy on the team with enough foresight to leave before things got crazy.

The others? They'd been caught when the cops showed up, and while the cops let them off with a warning, our coach... well, he'd sent us here.

To our very own personal hell.

"Let's get this over with," I said.

"That's the spirit," Ryan said as I led the way up the stairs to the front doors, the rest of the guys dragging their feet behind me.

"Maybe it won't be so bad," I added. "I mean, some pro players take ballet classes, right?"

"It's supposed to be good for flexibility," Cooper said.

"See? There you go," I said. "Maybe it'll be good for us."

"Couldn't we have just watched some YouTube videos or something?" Alex said from behind. "Do we really have to take classes?"

Ryan shook his head. "Have I taught you fools nothing?" He turned at the top of the steps to face the others, like he was about to make a speech. "Ballet classes are usually filled with girls, right? The way I see it, the coach did us a favor sending us here. Think of it like a field trip to hottie heaven."

I stared at him until he looked over. "What?"

I shook my head and opened the glass door leading to a sterile foyer. It smelled like cleaning products and I had to blink as my eyes adjusted to the dim lighting. I heard distant music and looked to my right to see a glass-lined wall so anyone in the entranceway could watch the dance class in action on the other side. The guys kept filing in behind me but I paused for a second at the sight of ten leotard-clad girls bending and stretching and—

Oof!

I'd taken a step forward to get out of the doorway and ended up tripping over something in my path. "Hey, watch it!" a girl's voice shouted.

No, not some*thing.*

Some*one.*

"I'm sorry," I said as I disentangled my arms and legs from the girl who was now sprawled out on the ground. I got a flash of an oversized black hoodie and long brown curls as I reached out to help her up. She turned to face me.

Ouch! She smacked my hands away as I tried to reach for her to help her up.

"I'm fine," she mumbled.

"Way to go, Ethan, taking out one of the dancers before we've even begun," one of the guys joked.

When we were both standing, she turned to face me with her hands on her hips and I fought the urge to grin. She was just so...little. And cute. Especially with that fierce scowl she wore like she was a little warrior about to do battle. "Can I help you?" she asked, though there was nothing hospitable about her tone.

"Yeah, uh sorry," I said, gesturing to the ground where we'd tumbled. "I didn't see you there."

She stared at me.

"I'm sorry," I tried again. "I really didn't see you."

"Nah, it was my bad," she said evenly, looking down at her hoodie and T-shirt. I followed her gaze and felt like the wind had been knocked out of me. It took all of my will power not to leer at the sight of her obvious yet hidden curves and rounded hips. "I must have forgotten to take off my cloak of invisibility," she finished.

Ryan choked on a laugh next to me as I dragged my gaze back up to see her watching me steadily, her eyes fathomless and unreadable.

I couldn't tell if she was teasing or really annoyed so I opted to ignore that comment altogether. "We're here for a, uh...ballet lesson?" Oh man, that sounded even lamer when I said it aloud. I looked around, distinctly uncomfortable under her watchful stare. "Is this the right place?"

She stared at me for another heartbeat, her lips twitching a bit before that placid, unreadable mask was back in place. "For ballet lessons?" She moved her head slowly and pointedly to the left where the dance class was still in session. Then she looked up at a large sign above a bulletin board announcing the ballet class schedule. When she looked back at me her big blue eyes were wide with feigned innocence. "Nope, no dance classes here. This is the post office." She shrugged. "Sorry."

Ryan was the only one to laugh. "Ethan, I think I love this girl."

'This girl' glanced over at Ryan and I could have sworn I saw a little smile.

What the...? So *Ryan* got a smile, and all I got was mocked? I tried not to feel jealous. I mean, obviously I wasn't jealous.

Why would I be jealous? I didn't even know this weird little girl.

"Look, if you could just tell us where we're supposed to be—"

The door to the classroom opened behind me. "What are these guys doing here?" a girl's voice asked. Suddenly our little band of brothers was surrounded by the leotard-clad girls we'd been watching through the glass. They were eyeing us with curiosity as they headed over to the girl in the hoodie, whose gaze hadn't veered away from me.

"I don't know," hoodie girl said. "They say they're here for a class."

"We *are*," I said, not loving the way she said 'they say' like we were suspect or something.

"Really." A pretty, tall blonde stopped beside the tiny warrior in the hoodie, turning in our direction with a sniff. "The most prestigious ballet academy in the Northeast, and we're now opening enrollment to...*these* people?" Her gaze moved over the lot of us and she pursed her lips when her gaze landed on Ryan beside me with his too-long hair and ripped jeans.

"These people," Ryan repeated softly. Turning to me, he said louder, "You were right. Ballet dancers are a bunch of stuck-up—"

"I didn't say that," I interrupted, my eyes seeking out the little brunette. "I never said that."

"Why not?" the brunette said. "It's true."

Ryan laughed and I couldn't stop a grin, especially when the snooty blonde rolled her eyes in irritation. "Ugh, *Collette*." The blonde turned to her with a sigh. "Don't encourage them."

So mystery girl's name was Collette. I mentally filed that away.

One of the other girls, shorter but no less skinny than the

rail-thin blonde, stood on the other side of Collette, partially hiding behind her as she eyed us. Her eyes lit on Cooper and her plain features turned pretty when she smiled. "Hi, Cooper."

We all turned to Cooper, whose expression hadn't changed. It rarely did. He was glowering at the timid, petite girl with the bun that looked painfully tight.

"You know him, Eve?" Collette asked.

Before Eve could respond the blonde turned to Collette. "Better question, how do you know them and why did you let them in?"

I took a step forward, ready to stand up for Collette, but I should have known she didn't need my help. "I didn't let them in. They walked in. This isn't a high-security fortress, it's a school. And as for how I know them..." She shot me a look. "I don't. One of them just ran me over."

I let out a huff of exasperated amusement. "I told you, I didn't see you there."

She opened her mouth to respond but the blonde beat her to it. "How could you miss her?"

As if her taunting tone weren't enough of a clue, I heard some of the girls beside us giggle. I looked over to see Collette hugging the hoodie tighter around herself, a splash of color in her cheeks.

"What are you guys doing here?" The question came from one of the girls to my left.

Before I got a chance to explain, a woman's voice came from behind us. "*I* invited them."

TWO

COLLETTE

Leave it to Mom to ruin my fun. I should have known she was behind the display of man meat standing in front of me. I mean, come on, there was no way the muscles on the guy called Cooper were homegrown. I was pretty sure whatever they were feeding the guys at Oakwood High wasn't on the FDA's approval list.

It had to be packed with hormones.

"Ms. Boucher, *really*?" Bianca whined in a pitch that hurt my ears.

She was standing next to me in all her five foot eight glory. Her stomach was flat. Her legs, long... I blinked, forcing my thoughts to something other than the fact that I was never going to live up to my mother's idea of the perfect ballerina. No matter how hard I tried, I was never going to cut it.

Ugh. I'd become envious of Bianca. What was *wrong* with me?

"You know Coach Reynolds?" Ethan asked. He'd finally stopped staring at me long enough to glance over at Amiee Boucher, aka my mom. Aka the serpent of the school.

Don't get me wrong, I love my mom. In a 'Harry Potter loves *he who shall not be named*' sort of way. You can't live with them and you can't live without them.

Mom nodded as she folded her arms and tapped her forearm. "I do. Although he said nothing about his team members storming my studio and interrupting our practice." I could feel the daggers Mom was shooting the other girls. The ones who were once practicing but now had gathered out in the hallway.

They all bowed their heads and murmured apologies as they disappeared back into the dance studio. The only people that remained were me—obviously—and Bianca—surprisingly. She never missed a moment of practice.

"Ms. Boucher, I really must protest. I mean, what if one of them drops us?" Bianca eyed Ryan who ran his hands through his hair and was leering at her in an obnoxious, *I don't care about the world* kind of way. It was intriguing, albeit a tad cliché.

But it made Bianca balk, and I knew right then and there, we were going to be friends.

"Why don't you come over here and we'll test it out," Ryan said.

Bianca's cheeks reddened as she cast a *see what I mean* look in Mom's direction.

Mom nodded. "Your objection is noted." She waved her hand in the studio's direction. "Now go practice. Your grand jeté needs work."

Bianca's lips parted and I could see how my mom's words crushed her. For a moment, I allowed myself to feel bad for her but then I remembered her taunt a minute ago about me and my weight, and that feeling magically melted into indifference.

Once we were Bianca-less, I glanced over at the team. Mom was assessing them in a way that made my skin crawl. I knew what it was like, having Mom stare at you. Judge you.

She sighed and waggled her fingers in their direction. "Come with me. I'll show you where you can change," she said as she started down the hall.

Everyone began to file after her. I stayed back, hugging my notebook to my chest and watching them leave. This was a major turn of events for me. Up until now, I'd lived a pretty boring life.

My job was to clean the studio. I was my very own Cinderella. At least, that was who I became as soon as the scale rose to the upper hundreds. That's when Mom suggested that maybe I would be happier on the sidelines. That I'd be happier if I didn't have to climb into a leotard every day.

That's when I was pretty sure I'd broken my own mother's heart. Any last hope she'd had that I'd fulfill her dream of being a perfect, ballerina daughter? It was officially gone.

I leaned against the wall and tipped my face toward the ceiling. I hated the tears that formed every time I allowed myself to think about ballet or Mom. I hated that I still wanted to dance. That it filled my soul and wouldn't leave me alone.

"Get a grip," I growled as I angrily wiped at my cheeks.

"Um..." a familiar voice drew my gaze over.

I glowered at Ethan as he stood awkwardly in front of me. He had his hands shoved into the front pockets of his pants and his ridiculously perfect brown hair had fallen across his forehead.

Of course he was perfect. His hair, shoes, even his exercise clothes. I hated his ridiculously perfect body he was so obviously *not* trying to hide underneath his white t-shirt and grey sweatpants. He didn't look like he even knew what "pinch an inch" meant and he most definitely did not have nightmares about it.

"What?" I asked, frustrated that I'd let my guard down. That this stranger had seen this part of me. Collette Boucher was the snarky, funny one. She wasn't the one who cried about her relationship with her mother or her weight.

"I, um..." He furrowed his brow as he stared at me. I widened my eyes as if that would hurry him along.

"I'm just making sure you're okay. I've been known to do some damage with my tackle."

I wasn't sure, but I felt as if he purposely flexed his pecs when he said that.

I snorted. "Seriously?" I slipped my notebook into my backpack and swung it onto my shoulder. I brushed my shoulder like I was flicking away a fly. "I barely felt you," I said.

Truth was, I was pretty sure he'd bruised my ribs, but I wasn't going to give him that satisfaction. This guy didn't seem like he needed any help in the ego department.

"Are you sure? I mean, sometimes you don't know you're hurt because of the adrenaline and blood rushing to the injury." He stepped forward and reached out to touch me.

Fear coursed through me and I flinched as I pulled away. I didn't want to be touched. I didn't want him to know exactly what I was hiding underneath this hoodie.

Ethan's eyes widened as he snapped his hand back. "I'm so sorry. I wasn't going to..." He pushed his hands through his hair as regret showed on his face.

I shot him a smile. "It's fine. I'm just not used to random guys touching me." I pushed the strap of my backpack higher up onto my shoulder and sidestepped him. "I should get going. Mom's waiting and she wouldn't be happy if I distracted you." It was a lame excuse but the only thing I could think of in a moment's notice.

Truth was, I had every intention of hiding out in Mom's office until this little practice was over. There was no way I wanted to spend my afternoon staring at Ethan as he bumbled his way through the different choreography.

It was a little insulting that Mom would take on these football players when she literally banned me from doing barre. That somehow, I was a disgrace to the art form that was ballet and these huge man-hulks were just what she was looking for.

I ducked my head as I made a beeline for Mom's office door when Ethan's voice stopped me in my tracks. I turned to see him staring after me.

"Aren't you going in there?" he asked, pointing toward the studio.

I shook my head. "Nope." I tucked my hair behind my ears and forced myself to keep my emotions in check.

He looked adorably confused. "So, you're not in this dance class or—"

"I don't dance." The words felt...wrong. It felt like a lie. Heck, it *was* a lie. I still danced on my own, I just wasn't welcome in dance classes...that my mother taught, at a dance academy. It was like living at Hogwarts, being Dumbledore's long-lost daughter, and not being able to practice magic.

And yes, I may have been rereading Harry Potter. Again.

"But isn't this, like...a dance school?" he asked.

For Pete's sake, why couldn't he just let it go? Mr. Perfect over here seemed intent on making me spell it out. I let out a weary sigh. "Yes, Captain Obvious, this is a school. It's a fully accredited high school as well..." I stopped myself before I could rattle off the whole brochure. He didn't need to know how competitive this place was to get into, or how expensive. I gestured behind me where my mother had disappeared. "That scary lady you just met? She's my mother."

"So you take classes here," he said.

"I take academic classes, yes," I said, beyond irritated that we were still having this conversation. "But I don't join in on the dance classes."

He looked so confused it was almost funny. "But you're the

ballet lady's daughter. Isn't following in your parent's footsteps like the reason your parents had kids?" And then his voice dropped and octave. "Or is that just mine?"

I shrugged as I turned. I didn't want to get into the nuances of my relationship with my mom or the fact that I have hips that disappointed her. I also didn't want to spill my guts to this stranger who was staring at me like I had two heads.

"Nope," I said over my shoulder and then disappeared into Mom's office and shut the door. Once I was alone, I settled down in her chair and tried to keep my gaze from slipping over to the window on the far wall. It allowed Mom to be able to watch what was happening in the studios without having to leave the comfort of her Aeron office chair.

I could see Mom had paired the partners together. Ethan was with Bianca—of course. As the two leaders of the group, it only made sense that they set the standard for what was expected.

Ryan was with Tilly and Cooper was with Eve. He was towering over her like King Kong towers over Ann Darrow. It was comical to see the two of them together. I half expected him to grab her and hoist her up the tallest building.

I chuckled at my own joke as I brought my feet up to rest on the seat of the chair. But that made my belly fat squish together so I dropped them to the floor and straightened.

Needing a distraction for the exact reason why I wasn't in the studio, fulfilling my family destiny like Ethan so delicately put it, I reached into my backpack and removed my notebook. I'd been working on my Harry Potter fan-fic—a secret obsession that I hadn't told anyone about, not even my best friend Olivia. It was a little embarrassing but it was fun and helped pass the time when I was stuck in the office, waiting for Mom to finish up.

Or when there isn't a studio free where I can let my guard down and dance.

I shoved the thought aside. Being in Mom's cramped office was better than doing what I loved. I just wished the hollow feeling in my chest agreed.

Eventually, I lost myself in my writing. I could always depend on the wizarding world to whisk me away. By the time my hand cramped, I glanced up to see practice was winding down. I straightened and set my notebook down on Mom's desk. Then I pressed my hand into my lower back, not realizing until now how cramped I felt.

Writing hunched over was wreaking havoc on my back.

Despite my best efforts, my gaze went directly to Ethan who was red faced and sweaty. I could tell from the way he was limping that Mom had not been gentle with this practice. She'd shown them what it was like to be a ballerina and they felt it.

Everywhere.

I allowed my smile to twitch on my lips. *Serves them right.* I could only imagine the jokes they told each other when they learned they were going to a ballet school. I'm sure words like '*sissy*' and '*girlie*' were thrown around a few times. The overly confident boys that first walked into the studio were now hunched over and shuffling out of the studio.

I was pretty sure they were eating their words.

I slung my backpack on my shoulder and moved to walk out of Mom's office. But, just as I reached out to grab the door handle, it swung open to reveal Mom's irritated expression.

"I know, Bianca, but there's nothing I can do. I made a commitment to their coach. They need to learn discipline and my dancers need to learn teamwork." Mom sidestepped me like I was a piece of furniture in her way. She set her clipboard down on her desk and pinched the bridge of her nose. She reserved that move only for Bianca when she was being a pain in the butt. Which was pretty much all the time.

"Ms. Boucher, I understand you made a commitment, but this is my career we're talking about. If I don't dance in the winter final, scouts won't see me. If scouts don't see me, I don't get into Juilliard." Bianca had her hands firmly planted on her hips.

Mom sighed and glanced over at her. "Rethink your statement, Ms. Jones. Every noun in there was *I*. Do you see why this school might have a teamwork problem?"

I stood in the corner, my gaze moving from Mom back to Bianca who looked like she'd just swallowed a lemon. I wished I had a bucket of popcorn and a soda, the drama was getting good.

Bianca sputtered a few times and then threw her hands into the air. "So that's it? There's nothing I can do?"

Mom turned to face Bianca, folding her arms across her chest. "There's nothing you can do about it. Not if you want to dance in the winter final."

I wanted to cheer and proclaim that the score was now Mom—one, Bianca—zero, but decided to keep my mouth clamped shut. I could sense the tone in the room and figured neither parties would be happy with my sudden outburst.

After an iceberg-melting stare from Bianca, she stormed out of Mom's office, nearly running poor Eve over in the process. I shot Eve a sympathetic smile as she steadied herself and then disappeared around the corner.

Mom's shoulders were tight when I turned my attention to her. She had her hands pressed down on her desk and I could tell she was stressed. It was the kind of stress that went beyond everyday Bianca drama.

Something else was going on.

"Everything okay, Mom?" I asked. There were very few

times I tried to reach Mom on an emotional level, but this felt like a heart to heart was needed.

Mom started and glanced over at me as if she'd forgotten I was even there. She cleared her throat and her moment of emotional weakness had passed. Ice Mom was back. "I'm fine." She sniffed. "Make sure the locker rooms are tidy. I've got work to do."

I nodded, feeling like a fool to try and give Mom my sympathy. Everything was work first, mother/daughter relationship later with her. I dropped my backpack in the corner. There was no way I was going to need it anytime soon. When Mom said she had work to do, that meant, *buckle up, we're staying the night.*

There was no way I was lugging my calculus book throughout the school.

"I'm on it," I said as I moved to slip from her office.

"Collette?" she asked.

I couldn't help but pause and turn my focus to her. "Yeah?"

Mom had sunk down into her chair and was rubbing her temples. "Order takeout please. We're going to be here for a while."

I saluted her and then stepped out into the hall. Cleaning the locker rooms would only take an hour. After that, I just might be able to sneak into one of the studios for a little R&R time to myself. I could turn on the music and lose myself in the movements.

With the way my shoulders were tight and stress had literally lodged itself into my joints, I needed the release dancing gave me. And for the first time all day, I felt excited.

Once everything was cleaned, I would dance my heart out.

Once everything was cleaned, I was finally going to be me.

THREE

ETHAN

A full twenty-four hours passed and yet I was still sore. Every muscle was screaming at me, and it didn't help that I'd had no time to rest. Coach still expected us to work our butts off at practice, not caring that we were in severe amounts of pain.

"I can't move, bro," Alex groaned as he walked into the locker room. "Somebody send for an ambulance."

At least I wasn't the only one suffering.

Cooper hissed as he sank down onto the bench beside me. "This is nuts, man."

I didn't try to argue because I agreed.

"How are we supposed to play Deerborn on Friday night if we can't move?" Ryan asked. He didn't sound particularly put out about it, more like he was musing over a philosophical question. Sprawled out on the bench across from me, Ryan stared up at the ceiling, his hands folded across his chest.

His question was a good one. How were we supposed to perform at our best if we were crippled with soreness after that excruciating dance workout? I'd tried to explain that to Coach Reynolds but he'd just given me that hard glare, his bald head glinting in the sun as he'd pointed to the field. "Stop your whining," he'd barked. "Get back to work."

I had the feeling any more complaining to Coach and our punishment would only get worse. The others knew it too, but that didn't stop them from griping to me, expecting me to do something about it. That was the price of being the team leader, I supposed.

One by one the guys finished up and headed out, until it was just me and Ryan in there. I was procrastinating, and I had a hunch Ryan was doing the same. He hated his home almost as much as I dreaded mine.

"Can I grab a ride?" he asked when I was packing up my bag.

Also, he needed a lift home. Unlike me and most of the other seniors on our team, Ryan didn't have a car.

"Yeah, sure," I said.

"You want to come over and jam with the band?" Ryan asked. "The guys are coming over in a half hour or so."

"Can't," I said. "My dad's gonna be home for dinner."

The rest went without saying. My dad was kind of a jerk—if he was going to grace us with his presence at dinner, then we all had to be there. No exceptions. Besides, if he got wind of the fact that I was using my precious free time to play guitar with Ryan's band, he'd totally lose it. If it wasn't football, schoolwork, or some other activity that would make the higher-ups at Yale take notice—it wasn't worth my time.

"Maybe this weekend," Ryan said.

I threw my dirty clothes into a laundry bin. "Yeah, maybe."

Probably not.

"I need you to listen to our new stuff," Ryan said, following me out of the locker room toward the parking lot. He smacked my arm making me wince. No part of my body didn't ache today. "Hey, did I tell you the news? We scored a gig at The Tailgate."

I stopped to face him. The Tailgate was an all ages club two towns over, and every band in the state wanted to get a spot in their lineup. "Seriously? That's awesome, dude."

He ducked his head. "Yeah, well. Tony's brother knew a guy..." Tony was the drummer, but even if he had connections, I highly doubted that would be enough to earn a coveted place in the lineup. The band was good, but Ryan was great. He wrote all the songs and was the singer and frontman, as well as the lead guitarist.

"Congratulations, man. You deserve it."

He shot me a little smirk. "I do, don't I?"

I shook my head. My best friend was a moron.

"You're going to come, right?" he asked. "It's in a few weeks."

"Of course," I said. *If my dad lets me.* That part was unspoken but understood.

I dropped Ryan off at his house and then headed home, walking in just in time to hear the tail end of my dad's call with one of his staff. My little sister Chrissy was perched on a stool at the kitchen counter and she gave me a smile and a wave when I walked in. Chrissy was twelve and a good kid. Super sweet but a little too sensitive—especially for this household. I tried to shield her from the worst of it, but my parents had what some might call a 'toxic' relationship. I wasn't sure why they were even still together, but I assumed it had to do with keeping up appearances. That was all that ever seemed to matter to both of them. In fact, it sometimes seemed like that was the only thing they had in common.

My mom was stirring something on the stove when I walked over and gave her a peck on the cheek. "Set the table," she whispered, so she wouldn't disturb my dad's call.

I dropped my bag near the kitchen door and moved past Chrissy to get out the silverware. The moment my dad ended his call, he turned to face me. "Good, you're home. Now we can eat."

No *hello* or *how was your day, son?* No one had time for niceties in this household.

"Elaine, is the food ready?" he asked.

"Almost," my mom said.

"Why isn't the table set?" He glared over at me and Chrissy, like this was an actual problem.

I held up the silverware. "Working on it."

"It would have been done by now if you'd come right home," he said, his tan, weathered face growing redder by the second as he worked himself up over nothing. Everyone said I was the spitting image of him, with my dark hair and tall build, but I sure as heck hoped that was where the similarities ended. "You were hanging out with your buddies, weren't you?"

Seriously, one would think 'hanging out with buddies' was some sort of criminal offense from the way he acted.

"Jack, leave the boy alone," my mother said, her voice mild and the words coming out by rote. This whole scene was basically performed on autopilot by all of us. We each had our roles to play in this family and none of us ever missed our cue.

"I'll get the water glasses," Chrissy said, right on time. My little sister was forever trying to please my parents.

I supposed I was, too, but as the eldest it wasn't always so easy. Nothing I did was ever good enough, especially for my father. I couldn't even come home from practice the way he wanted.

"Just don't be late on Thursday," my father continued. "We've got a dinner at the Falconers' house and they expect the whole family."

I stopped in the middle of placing a fork at my father's spot at the head of the table. The Falconers were the biggest donors to my father's re-election campaign, which meant they were *very important people* in my father's eyes. My dad was the mayor of this town and the upcoming election was the center of his universe. From the way he talked, one would think he was running for president and not for re-election as mayor of our little town. Technically, we were a small city, but no one in his right mind would consider this a thriving metropolis, more like an oversized suburb.

Dread knotted my stomach as I stood there staring at the place setting before me. Finally, I cleared my throat and lifted my head. "I don't think I'll be able to make it to the dinner on Thursday."

Everyone froze. Even my mother stopped fussing over the stove and turned to stare.

"What do you mean, you don't think you can make it?" My father's voice was calm. Too calm. Like the calm before a storm.

I tried not to notice the way Chrissy's face paled as she hovered at the counter behind him.

"I told you about Coach Reynolds' punishment, remember?"

My father's brows drew together in abject confusion, like I was suddenly speaking Greek. "What does that have to do with you? You didn't get into trouble at that party."

I cleared my throat again. "No, sir, but Coach still expects me to go to that dance academy since I'm the captain and—"

"That's horse hockey!" My dad didn't believe in swearing so 'horse hockey' was about as harsh as it got.

I shrugged. "I don't like it either, Dad."

"Did you talk to him about it?"

"I did."

"And?" My dad planted hands on his hips like he was about to face off with my coach right here and now.

"And...I couldn't get through to him."

The silence was deafening. This was just about the worst sort of failure on my part. My dad was a big believer that everyone in this family ought to be a leader. But unlike Coach, my dad's idea of being a leader didn't mean taking a punishment along with my teammates. It meant being able to persuade and command. *Persuade the powers that be and command the underlings*, that was one of his mottos.

"I tried, Dad," I said when I couldn't take the silence any longer.

"You tried." He shook his head. "Well, you didn't try hard enough."

I swallowed down a protest. It wouldn't do any good to argue. If anything it would make things worse. I focused instead on the way Chrissy was fidgeting with the forgotten and empty water glass in her hands, anxiety making her pale features tighten.

"I'll try talking to him again," I said, already dreading this conversation.

My father ignored this. "You're a Morrison," he said, as if I'd forgotten my own last name. "Morrisons don't take no for an answer."

He turned away, moving over to the refrigerator, no doubt to grab a beer for himself. I flashed Chrissy a reassuring smile but she still looked stressed.

Still facing the fridge, my dad droned on. "Morrisons don't give up, *we get things done.*"

That was another one of his famous mottos. I mouthed the last part along with my father behind his back, and finally got Chrissy to smile. She slapped a hand over her mouth to keep from laughing just as my father turned around to face me. "If Coach Reynolds won't listen to reason, then talk to someone else." He frowned. "Your time is valuable."

And he should know. My dad had every second of every day planned out for me, and had for as long as I could remember.

"Yes, sir," I said, relieved when my father turned to ask my mother about what we were having for dinner, officially putting an end to the conversation.

But one thing he'd said had gotten me thinking. If Coach Reynolds wouldn't listen to reason, maybe there was someone who would. Sure, the lady who ran the academy was equally terrifying in her own way, but it had seemed like she was just as unhappy about us being in her class as we were to be there. Maybe *she* would see reason—maybe I could get her to talk some sense into our coach.

It wasn't much of a plan but it beat the idea of wasting two evenings a week in a dance studio. I didn't tell the others what I was planning to do because I didn't want to get their hopes up, but the moment practice ended the next day, I took off for the academy.

I roamed the halls until the last of the girls filed out of the classroom and then I headed in, hoping I could find the teacher on her own.

I found someone all right...but it wasn't the teacher.

What I found when I walked into that studio—it took the wind right out of me. I had to reach out and steady myself against the doorframe as I watched her—this vision of grace and beauty as she glided across the floor, spinning and turning, her eyes closed like she was lost in thought.

Lost in a beautiful fantasy, judging by the way a smile turned up the corners of her lips and her expression turned dreamy.

She leapt and spun, moving across the floor like it was a lake and she was the swan, even though in my head, that sounded ridiculous and a little too sappy—even for me. But there was no other way to describe it.

I could have stayed there and watched her for hours. I had no idea how much time actually passed before she took off running—but not like a line backer was coming after her type of running, this was graceful and delicate—only to stop suddenly. Almost as if at the end of the dance floor, someone was supposed to be there to catch her and lift her up.

But she was alone.

She sighed and then giggled as she opened her eyes. I felt frozen, standing there, waiting for her to see me. I knew I should have run away. Left and never looked back. I mean, what kind of creep just stands there, watching a girl dance?

Apparently, me.

Before I could get my brain to command my legs, she turned and her gaze landed on me. It was strange, but suddenly, she seemed to be timid. Her body curled in on itself and she began shielding her body like I'd just walked in on her naked.

Collette's cheeks turned beet red as she glared up at me. "What are you doing here?"

FOUR

COLLETTE

This was bad. This was so very very bad.

What the holy loving crap was Ethan doing here? Staring at me with that goofy smile? How long had he been here? What had he seen?

I glanced down quickly as if to make sure that what I was wearing was indeed what I was wearing.

Yep. A leotard. And tights.

Well, Ethan now knew everything. Every lumpy, rolly detail of my life he was now privy to. There wasn't a part of my body that he wasn't intimately aware of now.

I wanted to cry. I wanted to curse. I wanted to hate him for interrupting my me-time. It felt as if he'd walked in on me while I was showering and instead of leaving, he decided it was best to just stand there and stare.

Every girl's dream. Exposing herself to a hot guy only to have her true self be so hideous that all he could do was gawk. Like I was a specimen in the circus.

I took the stunned look on Ethan's face as my cue to leave.

Reaching down, I grabbed my hoodie, threw it on, and hurried from the room.

Just when I thought I'd cleared the door, a hand wrapped around my arm and suddenly, I was being dragged back into the studio. I moved to speak, but I was too shocked.

One, that Ethan could actually move me. I knew he was strong, but I didn't think he was *that* strong.

Two, he didn't seem disgusted. Instead, he looked intrigued as he stared down at me.

I knew I should have been worried when I heard the sound of the studio door click shut. I should have run screaming from the room. I didn't know this guy. He could be a predator for all I knew.

But the realization that if I did run screaming, it would draw Mom's attention and then she'd *know* that I was hiding out, dancing in the studio, slammed into me. If Mom found out that would only elicit a long talk about body image and the expectations of a dancer. And I couldn't go down that path. Not again.

So I'd brave it out with this Ethan guy and just hope I could outwit him if he had some devious plot planned. It was already established that in a battle of strength, I would lose.

"What...I mean...how..." Ethan's stammering was sort of adorable. His cheeks were pink and his eyes wide. I could see flecks of yellow in his dark brown irises. They intrigued me and I found myself leaning in to get a better look.

Until I realized that I was the one leering, so I forced myself to pull away.

"What are you doing here?" I asked, tired of standing there, trying to decipher if Ethan was going to make fun of me or not. Ethan cleared his throat and then blinked a few times as if that was all it took to knock him from his stupor. His smile turned sheepish as he shoved his hands into the front pockets of his jeans.

"Sorry," he said.

Goosebumps rose up on my skin as I took in the depth of his voice and the way it sounded like he was flirting but in a stealth, James Bond sort of way. Which was so ridiculous to even think. Ethan didn't flirt with girls like me. He flirted with the Biancas of the world.

And then I felt stupid. Of course. That's why he was here. He was looking for Bianca.

"She's not here, you know," I said as I reached down and began to zip up my hoodie. I was trying to ignore the hurt that made my chest feel too tight. When did I become the sort of person that obsessed about a guy and what he thought about me?

It only ended in my heart being broken and the guy galloping away on his white horse with anyone else but me. I needed to get it through my head that girls like me never ended up with the guy. Period.

Ethan furrowed his brow as he leaned in. "And how do you know who I'm looking for?"

I scoffed as I wandered over to do barre and lifted my leg. I needed to stretch or I was going to feel it tomorrow. At least under the protection of my hoodie, I didn't have to worry about Ethan getting an eyeful.

But when I glanced over at him, his eyes were nowhere near south of the border. Instead, he looked quite amused as he studied my face.

I glared at him and then shrugged. "Because eventually, guys like you always come looking for girls like her." I leaned over my leg that was propped up on the bar. I could feel the stretch in my hamstring so I leaned closer.

"Wow. You're really flexible for someone who doesn't dance."

I glanced over at Ethan to see him staring at my leg. Worried that he was staring a little too long at my many flaws, I dropped my leg and turned so he was now at my back.

"You know who is really flexible? Bianca is really flexible. She's won the academy's highest award three years in a row." Great. Now I was babbling. And about Bianca. Why didn't I just set up a romantic dinner for them and call it quits?

"Bianca?" Ethan asked. He sounded more confused than certain and that caused me to look over my shoulder at him. Just as he met my gaze, I felt myself fall. I yelped and stumbled, bracing myself for the floor.

But it never came.

Instead, two very strong arms wrapped around me and I was suddenly weightless. My body stiffened when I realized, Ethan had lifted me up.

Oh no. Ethan had *lifted* me up.

I scrambled and pushed against him, desperate for him to put me down. It was one thing to guess my weight by looking at me. It was a whole other thing to verify your guess by holding me.

In my flailing, Ethan seemed to pick up on the hint and grunted as he lowered me to the ground. Once my feet were firmly planted, I straightened my hoodie and glared at him. He studied me with his eyebrows furrowed.

"Everything okay?" he asked.

My cheeks burned as I decided to drop to the hardwood and keep my stretching to a place where gravity couldn't betray me.

"I'm fine, why?" I asked.

Ethan glanced around and then sat next to me, wincing on

his way down. I studied him, wondering what that expression had been.

Once he was situated, he glanced over at me. "What?"

"What's with the wincing?"

He pulled one leg in while extending his other leg, just like I was doing. I giggled as I watched him lift his arms over his head and lean to the side.

His face flushed as he straightened and shot daggers my direction. "I'm—it's just that I'm dying here. I'm so sore that I can't even make it down half the field. Which, for the quarterback, is a bit of a problem."

I nodded as I pinched my lips. I'd expected that. "I'm guessing you didn't stretch after, did you?"

Ethan cleared his throat. "Not really into stretching."

I nodded as I stood and moved to stand behind him. I lifted his arms over his head and then pushed on his back so that his hands were nearly touching his feet. He groaned as I pressed into his shoulder blade harder.

"Stretching is important. For any sport," I said as I let up on his back and Ethan sprang back into place.

He nodded and then switched his legs and attempted the stretch on his own. He barely made it to his ankle. I shifted my weight and pressed my knee into his other shoulder blade.

"You know, for someone who doesn't dance, you sure know a lot about it."

There was a tugging on my heart with Ethan's words. It took a lot of effort to remind myself that I was not born to be a dancer. That it just wasn't written in my genetic code. And for the most part, I could accept that. That dancing was just going to be a hobby for me. Nothing more.

But there was something to the depth of Ethan's voice. Or the way he spoke about me and dancing like it was a no-brainer that allowed my soul to think, for just one moment, that he could be right.

I straightened to give Ethan a break and just as I did, I caught a glimpse of myself in the mirror.

And, that's why I live on Earth where reality reigns supreme.

"I never said I don't dance. I just said I don't take classes," I said as I left him to stretch on his own and settled back down next to him.

Ethan stopped moving and was staring at me. I could see his gaze from the corner of my eye. He was trying to figure something out and the obnoxious part of my brain wanted to know what that was.

"What?" I asked as I pressed my feet together and drew them inward. Then I cocooned over and rested my forehead on the floor.

"I'm just trying to figure you out," he said.

I tipped my face to the side so that I could meet his gaze. He had his hands extended behind him and was leaning back. He seemed to have given up on stretching as his legs were extended in front of him.

I sighed as I straightened. "Why? There's nothing special about me. I'm as boring as they come."

I hoped that he would take that response and leave it, but of course, he didn't.

"I doubt that. Boring people don't hide that they are incredibly talented at something." He raised his eyebrows and nodded toward my tights.

A warm, hot-chocolate feeling rose up inside of me at his compliment. He thought I was talented?

I mean, sure, he's a jock who rams into guys every Friday night. But he had stood there, watching me dance for an unspecified amount of time. That had to account for something.

But reality sucks and creeps up on you eventually. In the same moment that I allowed myself to feel excited that Ethan thought I was talented, I remembered that talent wasn't my problem. That it wasn't the reason why I wasn't enrolled in the academy.

And that reason was one that I'd been fighting my whole life.

Tears stung my eyes and that only angered me more. I was okay with my future and the lack of ballet in my life. I was okay with the fact that I was stuck on the sidelines, cheering for everyone else's future but my own. I was okay that I had to hide out in the studio to dance after hours.

I'd accepted everything about my future. Yet, all it took was one compliment from Ethan and suddenly, my resolve crumbled around me. I drew in a deep breath. "I'm not a dancer anymore."

His brows drew together in confusion. "If you're not a dancer, then...what was that?" He gestured toward the dance floor where I'd been rehearsing the routine that I'd never perform. Always the understudy, never the star. That was a saying, right? If not, it should be—it pretty much spelled out my life.

I followed his gaze, staring at the polished wooden floorboards like they might hold the answer. If I wasn't a dancer, why was I dancing? I shrugged. "That was just for me. For fun."

When I glanced over to look at him, the breath left my lungs in a rush. His dark eyes were filled with intensity. They were focused on me like I was the center of the universe. Like I was some amazing treasure he'd just discovered. I looked away first.

"I should get changed," I said as I moved to leave.

Ethan scrambled to stand and was over to me at a speed I would have never guessed he could produce. I mean, the man was built like a MAC truck and we all know how fast they are at getting up and moving.

"I have a proposal for you."

I paused, wondering if I heard right. "You what?"

He cleared his throat as he ran his hands through his hair. His lopsided smile caused my heart to pick up speed—only for a moment—before I shut that ridiculous reaction down.

"I'm thinking we could help each other." He pointed to my chest and then to his like I needed help remembering who 'each other' was.

I folded my arms as I stared at him. "And what could you possibly be able to help me with?"

He swallowed and then raised his hands up and moved them around. "With dancing. I noticed the last move you did required someone to lift you up." He dropped his hands to his side and shrugged. "I could do that."

Yes, he could. He'd already proven that. And it would be fun, finally dancing with a partner. Solos were great, but there were so many moves I'd wanted to try but had been unable to.

However, it would require him touching me. All. Over.

I scrunched up my nose and shook my head. "No thanks, I'm good," I said, turning to leave.

He moved—again with that speed—and situated himself in front of the door. "In exchange for my help, you can help me."

I paused and then glanced up at his ridiculously wide grin and knee-buckling dimple. I growled and reached around him to open the door. "What if I don't want to help you?"

Ethan leaned back, pressing his body weight on the door. "Well, that wouldn't be very nice."

I stared up at him as I attempted to pull the door open.

Even when I threw my weight behind it, I couldn't get it to move a centimeter. I was stuck in the studio until I agreed to whatever deal Ethan wanted to make.

So I sighed, blew away the loose strand of hair that had fallen from my bun and straightened. "What could I possibly have that you want?" I narrowed my eyes and placed my hands on my hips. And then I winced. "And please don't say the inside scoop on Bianca."

Ethan straightened as well, bringing him even closer to me. I caught a whiff of his cologne and his closeness was definitely awakening a part of me that I'd begun to doubt even existed. After all, there wasn't a line of guys waiting to kiss me. I'd all but given up that I'd ever be attractive enough to tempt a guy.

Startled and a little scared, I stepped back to give myself some space from the feelings that Ethan was eliciting. If he noticed my retreat, he didn't say anything.

I held my breath, waiting for him to respond. If he said Bianca, I was going to punch him. Right here. Right now.

He laughed. It was genuine and warm. And I liked it.

"I want nothing to do with Bianca, trust me. I know what girls like Bianca want." He shrugged. "I'm not that kind of guy."

I narrowed my eyes. "So what kind of guy are you?"

He held my gaze for a moment before he sighed and dropped his gaze to study the floor. I waited, wondering if I'd asked the wrong question. Just when I decided that I should try to walk back what I said, Ethan parted his lips and said something I never in a million years thought he would say.

"I want to play music."

FIVE

ETHAN

I waited for a laugh.

I mean, *I* would have laughed at me if I were her.

But a moment passed and there was no laughter. She just tilted her head to the side and studied me. "So, you're like...a musician?"

There was no mockery in her voice. No disbelief. Just curiosity. Almost like the idea wasn't totally insane. I shrugged. "I don't know. I wouldn't say I was a *musician*, I just...I like playing guitar."

Her lips twitched a little like she was on the verge of smiling. "I think that's called being a musician."

I let out a huff of laughter. I supposed she had a point, but I still felt weird admitting it. Ryan and the guys in his band were the only people who even knew I played, and yet here I was, spilling my guts to a girl I barely knew.

"So..." She drew the word out as her eyes narrowed on me. "What does that have to do with me?" She crossed her arms over her chest. "I know I *look* like a rock god, but trust me when I say I have no hidden talents with the guitar."

I laughed and was rewarded with a little smile in return. She arched her brows when I didn't immediately answer.

I opened my mouth and shut it, trying to figure out how to explain.

That was just for me, she'd said. *For fun.*

The words hadn't exactly been mind-blowing, and yet the moment she'd said it, I'd felt...jealous. That was the only word for it. Playing guitar was the only thing in my life that was just for me. I wanted to do it more, whenever I wanted. I wanted to play even if Ryan wasn't home. I wanted a place where I could stash my guitar and not feel like I was hiding some deep dark secret.

She was watching me expectantly, waiting for an answer.

"I need a place to practice," I said. I looked around at the empty studio. "It seems like you have an in here—"

She gave a little snort of amusement at the understatement. Her mom ran the place, after all. Surely she knew when the studio was free, and how to get in if it was locked.

"So maybe you could hook me up with the space, and I could help you when you need a partner," I said.

She pursed her lips. "Why can't you just play guitar at home?"

"Uh..." I shoved my hands in my pockets. "My dad would freak."

That was putting it mildly.

She stared at me blankly for so long, I started to fidget. "What?"

She gave her head a little shake like she was coming back to reality. "Sorry, I was just picturing your dad as the mean minister from *Footloose*. So, like...does your dad hate *all* music or just your music in particular?"

For what felt like the millionth time since I'd met her,

Collette's statement left me blinking in confusion. This girl never said what I expected her to say.

Maybe that was why I liked being around her so much. She was this odd, utterly unique little spitfire.

"I have no idea what you're talking about with *Footloose*, but the answer is neither. He doesn't even know that I play."

She pursed her lips, her hands on her hips. Finally, she said, "Explain."

If she were anyone else—or even if she'd phrased it any other way—I might have deflected. Come up with a half-truth to explain my situation. But with this girl, I just knew that half-truths wouldn't cut it. She spoke honestly and openly, and she expected the same in return.

"My dad's the mayor."

She didn't so much as blink, and her expression looked utterly unimpressed.

"He's also kind of a control freak," I said. "He has...*plans* for me." The man had my life mapped out until I was forty. Undergrad at Yale, law degree from Harvard, move back to this town and take over the law firm where he'd been a partner until he'd left to pursue politics. Join him in the Senate—because by then, he would have already been elected—where we would be the first father/son duo to take over the legislature.

I assumed at some point he'd find me the perfect wife—one who would provide me with the requisite two-point-five children who'd live in our home with its white picket fence.

"I assume his plans for you don't involve learning the guitar," she said.

"You assume right."

She did that head tilt thing again, like she was sizing me up, looking at me from a new angle. "So...what are *your* plans for you?"

The question felt like a sucker punch. It literally left me winded. It took me a second to realize why.

No one had ever asked me that before. Not just the way she'd phrased it, but the general gist of her question. I couldn't think of one person in my life who'd ever stopped to ask me what I wanted for my future. Not my mom, not my teachers, not my coach...and definitely not my dad.

She didn't wait for an answer, which was great since I didn't have one. I was still reeling from the weight of the question. What did I want?

"Do you want to be a musician?" she asked.

"I don't know," I said slowly. "I don't think so. I mean...I don't think I'm good enough."

She arched her brows as she considered that. "You're probably not. I mean, it does take ten thousand hours to master something. Even if you played every single second of every single day, you haven't even scraped the surface."

"You're probably right," I said.

"You need to practice more."

It was a valid point, but the more I thought about what she was saying, the more certain I was that I didn't want to make a profession out of music. It was the one thing in my life that gave me pleasure right now—even if it wouldn't make my dad go ballistic—to add that sort of pressure to it would defeat the purpose.

"My buddy Ryan," I said. "He's really talented. Like, natural talent. And he's obsessed with creating music..." I shook my head. "I enjoy playing, but music is more his thing."

She nodded, her expression thoughtful. Her arms were still wrapped around her middle, clutching that hoodie around herself like a robe. "So what's *your* thing?"

I stared at her in confusion. "What do you mean?"

She finally let go of her hoodie so she could flap her hands in impatience. "I mean, which house are you in? What makes you tick? What are you passionate about? What's your *thing?*"

"I—I don't know." Man, I felt so lame admitting that. But honestly, the only other response I could think of was 'being a good son' or 'playing football.' The first was pathetic and the second didn't ring true. I liked football. I was good at it. But it wasn't my *thing*.

She sighed and I had this feeling that I'd disappointed her with that answer.

"You don't *know?*" She sighed. "Are you *always* this obtuse or is that just a jock thing?"

"I don't know," I said, torn between irritation and amusement. "Do you *always* feel the need to reference Harry Potter or is that just a geek thing?"

Her lips hitched to the side and her eyes lit with amusement. "You caught that, huh?"

I moved forward a bit until I was so close I could reach out and touch her. This time she didn't backpedal away from me, which I took to be a win. "Cloak of invisibility? Which house are you in? Yeah, I caught that."

Her lips did that twitching thing again. "You've read Harry Potter?"

"Please," I scoffed. "I'm an athlete, not a heathen."

Her eyes widened and then she let out a laugh. An honest-to-goodness laugh.

That laugh was *everything*. My heart freakin' swelled in my chest and I had to fight the urge to pull her into my arms. Instead, I shoved my hands into my pockets again.

"To answer your question," I said when her laughter faded. "I honestly don't know my *thing*. I guess that's why I want some space to call my own." I looked around the studio pointedly. "Some place where I can maybe...start to figure it out."

She was quiet for a long moment. "To answer *your* question, no."

I arched my brows, trying not to feel too disappointed. "No?"

She shook her head slowly. "No, I don't always reference Harry Potter." A mischievous little smile tugged at her lips. "Sometimes I reference cheesy eighties movies, too."

My laugh was filled with relief. She wasn't saying no to me sharing her studio space. That was something.

She still wore that small smile, and for a second our eyes met and held. She was so pretty, especially when she smiled. And right now, it felt like there was something here between us. Some sort of connection that I couldn't name.

I didn't want this to end…I didn't want to stop talking to her, and I just knew that any second now she'd walk away. "What's your thing?" I asked.

She blinked like I'd startled her. "What?"

I gave her a teasing grin. "Your thing," I said. "What is it? I mean, if it isn't dance—"

Her smile faded fast and while I had the distinct feeling I was putting my foot in my mouth, I was also curious as to what was going on with this girl. "You're so talented," I said, glancing toward the dance floor again. "And you clearly love to dance, so…"

I trailed off, waiting for her to explain.

Her stare slowly turned into a glare as the silence between us grew tense. "You're really going to make me spell it out for you," she said.

I blinked in surprise at the sudden bitterness in her voice. "I guess I am."

She sighed loudly as she looked down at herself. Looking back up at me, she gave me a humorless smirk. "I'm not built for the part."

She was basically inviting me to look at her body, and my mouth went dry as I took her in. So beautiful, so curvy, so... sexy. I tore my eyes away and saw her scowling at me, waiting for some sort of response.

"I, uh...I don't get it."

She huffed but the pink in her cheeks made it clear her annoyance was more out of embarrassment than anything and that made me feel like a jerk. I wasn't trying to humiliate the girl, I just wanted to understand.

"Can you imagine *me*, flitting around like some delicate butterfly?" Her voice dripped with sarcasm. "I'd look ridiculous."

"You looked perfect." I cleared my throat. I just didn't know what to say when girls talked about themselves and their bodies. Was I supposed to compliment her or agree? Why did women have to be so complicated?

If I was going off of instinct, then my inner guy wanted to tell her she was crazy. I'd watched her earlier. She was mesmerizing. Way more interesting to watch than a butterfly. And in the sex appeal department, she won the pot. But I knew for certain, a girl I'd just met wouldn't be too happy if I said that.

So I stuck with my initial response and waited for her to speak.

She opened her mouth and then clamped it shut again and I was horrified to see pain in her eyes.

"I saw you, remember?" I gestured toward the dance floor. "You looked perfect."

"Well, I don't look like Bianca." She muttered it under her breath, but I still heard it and the mention of that prissy blonde beanpole made me irrationally angry.

"Why are you so obsessed with her?"

Her eyes widened for a second at the anger in my voice.

Then she shrugged as if the answer were obvious. "She's everything a ballerina is supposed to be—pretty, elegant, thin."

Her voice was filled with disdain and...something else. Something rueful and disparaging, but not toward Bianca. She was hating on *herself*.

I took a step closer, needing her to see my sincerity. She kept her gaze focused straight ahead so she was staring at my chest. I reached out and tipped her chin up with one finger so she was forced to look at me. "And you are graceful, unique, and....*beautiful*."

Her eyes widened, and I...I was an idiot. I'd said too much. I'd been too earnest.

But I'd meant it.

My heart was thudding painfully in my chest, my blood roaring in my ears as I waited for her to respond. When she didn't speak right away, my entire body went cold.

Seriously, what was I doing? I barely knew this girl. She was basically a *stranger*. A stranger who now knew that I played guitar, who knew about my dad's control freak ways, and a stranger who was staring at me like I'd just lost my freakin' mind.

Maybe I had.

I didn't even recognize this guy who'd spilled his guts to a girl he didn't know. And I definitely couldn't explain why I'd felt the need to touch her, to comfort her, to...freak her out, apparently.

In those big blue eyes all I saw was shock and confusion before she shut down on me, and then I couldn't read any emotions at all.

I dropped my hand from her chin, breaking the tense moment. She took a step back, looking away from me. "I don't know why I'm talking to you about this," she said. "You wouldn't understand."

And then she was walking away from me, hurrying toward the door like I was going to chase after her...again.

I wanted to—we definitely weren't finished here. But this time I let her go.

When she reached the door to the studio, I called after her. "So? Do we have a deal?"

She didn't look back but she paused with one hand on the handle. "I'll think about it."

SIX

COLLETTE

Olivia knew something was up the next day at lunch. She kept staring at me as I pushed my chicken Alfredo around on my plate. I knew I should have picked up a salad or stuck to a Diet Coke, but I was hungry or depressed or just in need of some warm comfort, so I'd risked the judgy look from the academy's cafeteria lady and gone with the carb load.

Of course, that had been a dead giveaway to my current state of mind, which was why I was getting sidelong glances from my best friend.

"Are you sure you're feeling okay?" she asked. She was eating her regular bagel slathered in cream cheese. Like many of the girls at this school, she had the body of a pixie and the metabolism of a horse. Carbs weren't *her* enemy. She took a bite, all the while eyeing me.

I sighed and pushed my pasta away. I wasn't in the mood to eat. Not after my encounter with Ethan last night. It had left me feeling raw and exposed and I knew I should be used to feeling that way, but what he'd said—no other human had ever uttered to me. This was uncharted territory.

"What would you do if a guy called you...graceful, unique, and beautiful?" The last three words barely made it from my lips. It was like my body was physically stopping me from saying those things about myself.

Olivia dropped her bagel and turned her entire focus on me. "I'm sorry, what?" She closed her eyes for a moment, took a deep breath, and then leaned closer as she stared at me. "Who is the guy and does he have a best friend?"

I squirmed in my seat as I reached out to pick up my tray. "I didn't say anyone said that to me. I'm just wondering, what would you do?"

Olivia narrowed her eyes, her tight black curls bobbing as she leaned forward, resting her elbows on the table. "So this is a 'you're stuck on a deserted island, what do you bring,' type of situation? You're honestly telling me you're not talking from experience?"

I winced, not wanting to lie to my best friend, but I also didn't want to tell her about Ethan quite yet. Besides, she was always telling me to love myself and take what my mom said and shove it where the sun don't shine. She might have been a dancer, but she hated the body shaming that came along with being a ballerina. She couldn't figure out why someone would starve themselves just to get into a leotard and jump around the stage—her words, not mine.

Call me crazy, but if I had two people in the span of twenty-four hours telling me how wonderful and beautiful I was, I thought I might explode. Like, *BOOM*, bye-bye Collette.

And honestly, I still didn't quite know what Ethan's angle was. My latest guess? This was all part of some elaborate high school prank. Or maybe a hazing ritual. He could have been sent to this school to get me to have feelings for him, only to pull the rug out from under me.

Was I being paranoid? Possibly. Okay, definitely. But my gut was telling me I had to be on my guard.

"That's what I'm telling you," I said as I pinched my lips together and willed my cheeks to stop giving me away. Was I ready to share Ethan with her? I wasn't sure.

And maybe there was a part of me that thought if I did say something, speak his name out loud, reality would kick in and I would wake up only to discover that I'd been living in some sort of dream.

And maybe I wasn't ready for that dream to end.

Olivia gave me a look that rivaled my mother's. She didn't believe me, her narrowed eyes and pursed lips told me that, but thankfully, she wasn't going to push it more.

"If a guy told me all of those things I think I would marry him. On the spot. No questions asked." Olivia picked up her club soda and took a sip. "Why? What would you do?"

I blinked a few times. Her direct question startled me. I shrugged and took a drink of my water—I needed a minute to mull my response over. By the time it became apparent that I was going to need to answer her, I settled on, "It would never happen to me so it's a moot point." I shot a smile in her direction as I slipped my backpack on my shoulder and stood.

I leaned forward to grab my food tray and turned—only to have someone barrel into me, flipping the tray upwards, and dumping my uneaten pasta all over my baggy sweatshirt.

"What the—" I glanced up to see Bianca's irritated stare.

"What are you *doing?*" she snapped. "Don't you ever look where you're going?" She sighed as she sidestepped me, pausing for a moment to make a point to stare at my lunch choice, which was slowly sliding down my chest. "And carbs? Really, Collette? It's like you don't even try."

She left before I could sputter out a reaction. The only thing I managed was an icy glare...at the back of her head.

Frustrated with my complete lack of a comeback, I set my tray down on the table, tipped myself forward, and scraped the now congealed noodles off my clothes.

"Why do you let her talk to you like that?" Olivia asked as she stood as well, handing me her remaining napkins.

I fought the tears that were threatening to spill. There was no way I was going to let anyone see just how hurt I was by what Bianca said. Worried that I would lose control over my emotions, I just shrugged. "She's a witch," I mumbled out as I set the soggy napkins on my tray.

This time, I made sure no frantic dancer was headed my way. Luckily, there wasn't. I walked over to the garbage and dumped my food into it. *Serves me right, ordering fettuccine Alfredo.* I had a feeling an empty can of Diet Coke would have done much less damage.

Now, I was going to smell like parmesan cheese all day long.

"Bianca is a witch with a capital B. Where was she rushing off to, anyway?" Olivia asked. "It's not like anyone is just dying to talk to her."

I shrugged as I waited for Olivia to throw her lunch away as well. I held onto my backpack strap as I glanced around. It was a testament to how distracted I'd been by Ethan's words that I only now actually noticed my surroundings. The cafeteria was surprisingly empty. Normally, it was packed with hungry dancers during the lunch break. But today? It was like a ghost town.

"Where do you think they all went?" I asked.

Olivia turned around and shrugged.

Olivia was a talented dancer, but she was far more interested in studying choreography than becoming the dance world's next prima ballerina. While her parents wanted her to have classic training, she was just biding her time until she could move to New York or Los Angeles and pursue her true passion, modern dance.

This was on the downlow, of course. My mother would have lost her mind if she knew that one of her precious ballerinas wasn't passionate about ballet.

"Wherever they've all gone off to, Bianca was in a hurry to join them," Olivia said. "That alone tells me we don't want to be there."

Olivia hated Bianca almost as much as I did. Easy to do, really, when her general attitude made the Wicked Witch look like an angel.

I ignored the comment, because this little mystery gave me something to focus on that was not Ethan. Also, I really hated not knowing what was going on, "Come on, let's go see where they all ran off to," I said, not really waiting for her to respond as I took off in the direction Bianca had headed.

Olivia sighed, but she followed along behind me.

"It'll only take a minute and then we can head to chem," I said as I started down the hallway that led to the dance studio.

"One minute," she said as she fell into step with me. "And I'm only going so I can give Bianca a piece of my mind. I don't know who she thinks she is talking to my best friend like that."

"Just ignore her," I said. "That's what I do."

Olivia huffed. "Yeah, but you have to take the high road since your mom runs this place. I mean, heaven forbid you incur the wrath of the school's biggest donor."

"Exactly." My mom never outright said it but it was understood that we both had a job at this school. Hers was to run it, and mine was to keep my head down and make life easier for everyone around here. That meant chipping in with cleanup and laundry duties, helping with some office work, and—most importantly—not making enemies out of the spoiled brats this school relied on for money.

My mom and I might have had our issues, but we were still a team. After my dad left and it was just the two of us, we became more like partners in a lot of ways. Which was why it was still nagging at me that she'd been stressing over something lately and not telling me about it.

"You know, half the time, I don't even know what she's doing here," Olivia grumbled, interrupting my thoughts.

I looked over at her in surprise. "Who...Bianca? She's the most ambitious dancer in the school."

Olivia shrugged. "Yeah, I know. It's just that she's always so miserable."

"Yeah," I agreed. "I don't know...maybe she's just a miserable person."

As I said it, my mind called up an image of Ethan as he'd talked about his dad and all the pressure he was under at home. For a second there, I'd genuinely felt for the guy. No matter what his motives in calling me beautiful...I didn't doubt that he'd been honest about everything else.

All he wanted was to play music. And if anyone could understand needing that kind of outlet, it was me. I let out a long exhale as I realized, I didn't really have a choice. If Ethan needed a place to play, I'd help him.

Oblivious to where my thoughts had gone, Olivia launched into a tirade about how Bianca was going to get a massive wake-up call one day once karma kicked in.

I hoped she was right, but I wasn't banking on it.

I reached out and threaded my arm through Olivia's as we drew close to the dance studios. I was grateful for her support. She always seemed to know exactly what I needed. When I needed a wing-woman, she would always step up to the plate.

I pushed open the large doors that separated the school from the academy. I could hear giggling and whispers as I made my way down the hall to Mom's office. All the dancers were clustered in front of the bulletin board—Bianca was at the center of them.

We stopped on the outskirts of the semicircle, but I couldn't make out what they were all staring at. Thankfully, Eve had wiggled her way out of the crowd and I flagged her down.

"What did Mom post?" I asked.

Eve's eyes were wide and her cheeks flushed. Excitement flitted around in her gaze as she studied me. "Apparently, some scouts from Juilliard are coming to pick a dancer to perform with the company this fall." Her voice was breathy and she hung onto me like she would float away if she let go.

I almost laughed out loud. The thought of me being an anchor—hit home a little too hard.

"So..." Olivia asked as she leaned in.

One of the taller girls in front of me shifted and I could read the announcement for myself. "So, everyone in the academy is going to get a chance to perform in front of the most prestigious dance school in the country," I whispered.

Eve squealed as she tightened her grip on my arm. "This is just what I need. An opportunity like this will only solidify my chances for a scholarship next year." She looked to me and Olivia, her expression was filled with hope, but her eyes held a hint of desperation. "Right?"

I nodded. "Yeah, definitely."

"For sure," Olivia added, her voice filled with encouragement.

Eve wasn't like Bianca. Or Olivia, for that matter. Eve's family didn't have the funds to send her here. To buy her way in. Every semester, she had to prove her worth to the school or they would pull her funding.

I couldn't imagine the kind of stress she was under. If I met the requirements to be a ballerina, I was a shoo-in. Mom wouldn't settle for anything less.

"Are you going to try?" Olivia asked, pulling me from my thoughts.

I glanced over at her, confused about what she was asking. "Am I going to try what?" I asked as I tucked my hair behind my ear.

"Try out. It's for everyone, right? I mean, why not you?"

My cheeks heated as a few of the younger dancers that were within earshot glanced over at us. I wanted a hole to open up and swallow me as I felt their gaze drop to my body—that was covered in Alfredo sauce.

If I didn't look like a pig before, I certainly did now.

Desperate to get out of here before word made its way up to Bianca that I was considering trying out, I grabbed onto Olivia and pulled her from the crowd. We made our way back to the school side of the building, the door shutting with a resounding thud.

"Man, those girls," Olivia muttered under her breath. "It was like I'd suggested you blow up the school or something." She glanced over at me with a sympathetic smile and that just made me feel worse.

I shrugged as I reached up and began pulling my hair into a ponytail on the top of my head. What did I care what those girls thought?

Sure, they were my peers. And yes, they knew just as much about dancing as I did. And maybe they did have a sliver of realism when they looked at me and gave me that *are you joking* look.

I knew dancers. I knew what they had to do to maintain their perfect figure. A lot of them had given up cake and cookies. I bet most hadn't had a milkshake in a decade. Some of them had been on hard-core diets for as long as they could remember.

All of them had spent a lifetime training and working and compromising and making sacrifices, in some form or another.

So they knew what it was like. And they knew the cutthroat competition that would take place now that something as big as Juilliard was coming to our small academy.

For me to stand there, in my size, daydreaming about trying out and worse, imagining that I could even win? Well, I would stare at me too.

I sighed as I shrugged and threaded my arm through Olivia's. "Let's not talk about it anymore."

Olivia and I began walking down the hallway to the chem lab. The bell was about to ring and there was no way I wanted to be late. If I couldn't have Juilliard, then I needed the grades if I hoped to get into a good college.

Olivia was quiet for a few seconds before I felt her take in a deep breath. I braced myself for her response. But, nothing came. Instead, I felt her relax as we both walked into chem just as the bell rang.

I blew out my breath as soon as I dropped onto my seat. I took a second to calm my racing mind. My heart was pounding, even if I didn't want to admit it.

There was a part of me that wished, deep, deep down, that I had the courage to try out. That maybe, just maybe, I might have a chance. That I might prove to my mom and the whole ballet community that I was good enough to dance.

That if they looked past their preconceived notions about what beauty and grace were, they just might find the talent that resided in me.

Maybe for the rest of the day, I was going to tell myself that I would try out. That I would be brave. Thinking about it wasn't going to harm anyone, and when I thought those things, I felt happy.

And was it so wrong to feel happy? Just for a couple of

hours. And then I would return to reality. I would return to my future.

A bleak, depressing, ballet-less future.

But until then, I was going to live my dream. Besides, who would it hurt?

Maybe me.

But I was okay with that.

I was used to being hurt.

SEVEN

ETHAN

I was sitting in the same studio as last night, but it couldn't have felt more different. Rather than just me and Collette standing here in relative silence, the room was now filled with unhappy football players on one end and miserable-looking ballerinas at the other.

We were all doing leg stretches on the floor as we waited for Collette's mom to show up and lead this class. Well, everyone else was waiting for Ms. Boucher.

I was waiting for Collette.

I knew she wasn't in this class, but that didn't keep me from looking for her. Every time the door opened, my head snapped up to see who it was. It was stupid, but I kept expecting her to walk in the door and give me crap for how inflexible I was or how I ought to be stretching more in my off hours. But mainly, I was waiting for her to tell me yes or no.

"Dude, are you even listening to me?"

I looked over to see Ryan watching me oddly and I realized he'd been talking for a while and I hadn't heard a single word. "Sorry," I said. "What did you say?"

"Man, you've been out of it all day, what's with you?"

I looked away because I knew he was right but I didn't want to explain that all day all I'd been able to think about was Collette. I couldn't stop thinking about last night and this potential deal I'd proposed to have access to some studio space.

I hadn't even realized how much I wanted it until I'd put it out there. And now—now it was everything I wanted. Just a place where I could go and...do my thing, as Collette put it.

Last night with Collette had been...well, it had been intense. But it had also been real. This might sound a tad pathetic but last night I'd felt like myself for the first time that I could remember.

For years now I'd been going through the motions—being the teammate and leader I was supposed to be, the son I'd been raised to be, and the student my teachers expected me to be.

It was killing me. I didn't realize how much I'd been creating the life my father wanted me to create until last night when I'd stopped. And I'd talked. And I'd told someone what actually made me happy.

Not someone—Collette.

And the crazy part? She hadn't laughed.

But she hadn't said yes to this crazy plan either, so...I was stuck in limbo, I supposed. And until I saw her, until I talked to her—I was pretty much useless.

"Does your weirdness have to do with your meeting with the coach?" Ryan asked.

"Nah, man, it's just a bad day, that's all."

He didn't say anything, and I was glad he hadn't tried to cheer me up. The whole team had heard the coach ream me out about my lack of focus on the field today. When he was done publicly humiliating me, he'd called me into his office. I would've preferred more red-faced hollering instead of the talk we'd had. I'd seen actual pity in his eyes when he told me how he'd gotten a call from my dad. Seemed my father hadn't taken my word for it that I'd handle the whole ballerina situation and he'd gone ahead and taken matters into his own hands.

"So, you're going to pull me from the ballet classes?" I'd asked.

Coach had snorted with amusement. "Heck, no. I explained to that hothead father of yours that college scouts would love the fact that you were going above and beyond to improve." Coach had waved a dismissive hand. "He came around eventually."

I'd been oddly grateful. I still was as I sat here hoping to catch a glimpse of Collette. I mean, I still didn't love the idea of putting my body through the torture that was ballet class, but I did love the idea that classes could be the perfect excuse to escape my house and take a little time to do something for myself.

"So, what do you think, man?" Ryan asked.

"What do I think..." I repeated stupidly.

He groaned. "You're not listening at all, are you?"

I didn't try to deny it as I dropped my head, forcing myself to stop staring at the door. She wasn't coming. I tried not to be too disappointed. I mean, she hadn't said *when* she'd let me know, right? But even so, I'd snuck my guitar out to my car this morning before I'd left the house. Tonight would be the perfect night to start our practice sessions since my parents would be out until late. I'd hoped she'd have given me an answer by now, but then again I was the idiot who hadn't given her my number so she could text me, or—

Ryan smacked my arm. "I said, we *need* you."

I looked over at him and blinked. "Um...need me for what, exactly?"

Ryan rolled his eyes, leaning back against the wall, not even pretending to stretch. "You didn't hear anything I just said, did you? I was saying that Keith had to bail on the gig at The Tailgate next month. We need a stand-in guitarist." He arched his brows. "You in?"

"Yeah." I didn't stop to think. I didn't have to. My heart had started pumping at the very idea of playing in front of people. And to play with Ryan and his crew? At The Tailgate? This would be epic. No way I'd miss it. "Of course, man. Absolutely."

He grinned at my enthusiasm and I tried to focus on the details he started rattling off rather than what lies I'd have to come up with to get out of the house.

"Ms. Boucher can't make it." Bianca the uptight blonde stood over me and Ryan, her hands on her hips as she scowled down at us.

"Great," Ryan said in his laziest, I-don't-give-a-crap tone. "Does that mean we get to go home?"

Bianca kicked his foot. "No, moron. It means that I'll be leading class."

"Where's Ms. Boucher?" Eve asked. She was hovering beside Cooper, who looked like he wasn't even aware of her existence as he checked something on his phone.

During the first class, Collette's mom had paired us up, assigning one of the ballerinas from her top class to each of us football players. They were supposed to help us, and none of the ballerinas tried to hide the fact that they viewed this as an extreme form of punishment.

Bianca had been the loudest of them all with her complaints so it must have been killing her to not only have to participate in this class, but lead it.

"Will she be coming later?" one of the other girls asked when Bianca ignored Eve.

"How should I know?" she snapped. "I ran into Collette in

the hall and she passed along the message. She said her mom had a meeting with the board of trustees."

"Is it about the Juilliard audition?" one of the girls asked.

I'd stopped listening the moment Bianca had said Collette's name. I turned toward the door again. She was out there. Was she waiting for me?

Suddenly Bianca was right in front of my face, blocking my view of the door. "Are we keeping you from something, Mr. Morrison?"

Ryan gave a low whistle behind me. "Wow, Bee. Are you always this much fun or did we just catch you on a good day?"

One girl giggled behind me, and Bianca's frown deepened. "Why are you even here, Ryan? It's clear you don't care about any of this."

"News alert, Queen Bee." He gestured around to the team. "None of us care about ballet, we're just here because our coach is making us."

"Oh, but we were just dying to get stuck teaching a bunch of meatheads remedial footwork," she shot back, her tone dripping acid. "That's not at *all* a waste of our precious rehearsal time."

"Is your bun too tight, Bee? Is that why you walk around like you've got a stick up your butt?" Ryan sounded genuinely confused and I caught Eve trying valiantly not to grin.

Bianca's scowl was terrifying as she leaned in until her nose nearly brushed his. "Just try to keep up."

I heard Ryan's soft laughter behind me as Bianca whipped around and headed toward the front of the room.

My body was in motion before I even totally knew what I was doing.

"Where are you going, man?" Cooper asked. His question drew Bianca's attention but I was already at the door when she spoke.

"Ethan, where do you think you're going? We're about to start." Bianca called after me in an irritated tone that gave me a sort of satisfied feeling. I hated the way Collette seemed to bow down to this girl. Like, somehow, Bianca was better than her.

"You guys start without me," I said, one hand on the door handle. "I've, uh...there's something I have to do real quick."

"Eth—" Bianca started.

But I was already out the door, turning to head down the hall and—

Almost ran right into Collette.

I stopped short just in time, but the look she gave me while sitting cross-legged by the studio door was absurdly smug. "You need to look where you're going."

I crossed my arms and looked down at her. "And you need to stop sitting on the floor."

She pursed her lips like she was thinking that over. "Touché." She started to get to her feet and I reached a hand down to help her. She paused for a second, looking at my hand like she wasn't sure what it was before continuing to her feet without my help.

It stung a bit, that she didn't take my help, but I brushed it off. We were friends. "So, what are you doing out here?" I asked.

She smirked as she shoved a notebook into her bag. "Waiting for you, obviously." She glanced over at the studio door. "What are you doing out here?"

"Looking for you. Obviously."

She grinned and for a second I couldn't quite remember how to breathe. Something about bringing air in and pushing it out. Her smile was unnervingly sweet, a distracting counterpoint to all her sarcasm and snark. It made me feel off balance.

"Bianca's going to kill you if you skip class," she said.

"I don't care about Bianca."

Her lips pressed together like she was trying not to laugh. "That won't stop her from murdering you."

"I'll take my chances."

"Ooh, you're a rebel," she teased. "I like that."

"So?" I said. "What did you decide? Are you gonna help a guy out?"

She sighed and tucked her hair behind her ear. "This is just about me dancing and you playing, right?"

"Yeah, that's the deal."

"And you promise to show up? Make this a priority?"

"Of course." Everything in me tensed as I waited for her answer. I had a feeling she knew it too, because the silence dragged on too long, and her expression was way too smug.

She was kind of adorable when she was smug.

Finally, with a sigh, she said, "Oh all right, we have a deal."

My heart gave a weird jolt, like a kick to my ribs. I was doing this. I was defying my dad, I was playing guitar...and I was doing it with Collette.

"Why are you looking at me like that?" she said, her tone suspicious as she turned her head to give me an assessing sidelong look.

"Like what?"

"Like I just told you you've been accepted into Hogwarts."

I arched by brows. "Really? That was a stretch, even for you."

She threw her hands up. "You shouldn't have called me out on my Harry Potter references. I warn you now, I was holding back before."

"Oh no," I groaned, going along with her teasing. "You're going to be unbearable now, aren't you?"

"Sorry," she said with a shrug that said she wasn't sorry at all.

"So, when can we start?"

"Tonight work for you?"

It was hard to play it cool, but I managed. Sort of. "Tonight works great," I said just a little too quickly.

"After you run home to grab your guitar, you can meet me back here."

"I have my guitar in my trunk," I said, totally forgetting my plan to play it cool.

Her brows shot up. "How very optimistic of you."

I mimicked her sorry-not-sorry shrug. "I just know I'm impossible to refuse."

She let out a loud laugh that had me grinning and the door behind us bursting open. "Ethan Morrison, what do you think you're doing out here?"

I turned to see Bianca scowling, her icy blue gaze shifting from me to Collette and then back again. "We're waiting on you."

"I'll be right in."

That was obviously not the answer she'd been hoping for and she turned her glare to Collette. "Why are you distracting him? Don't you have somewhere to be?"

"Nope." Collette's voice sounded too cheery and her smile was way too bright.

Bianca's sigh was weary as she turned to me. "Can we please just get this class over with?" She glanced over at Collette. "*Some of us* have an audition for Juilliard to prepare for after this."

Collette's smile never faded, but everything about her dimmed with that comment. The light in her eyes went out, and she seemed to lose an inch of height as her shoulders slumped.

I gave her a questioning look, but I knew better than to ask why she allowed Bianca to act like that with her. But I figured she didn't want to get into the details, not with Bianca hovering nearby. I filed it away as something I would bring up later.

Collette ignored my stare. "That's fine," she said to Bianca. "We were just finishing up out here."

Bianca seemed to take that as a win and she turned to head back into the classroom. "Come on, Ethan. They're all waiting."

I moved to follow, but I paused in the doorway and leaned back out to look at Collette. "Where should I meet you tonight?"

She opened her mouth, but I knew what she was going to say.

"And please don't say platform nine and three quarters."

"You are no fun at all." She bit her lip, her eyes twinkling in mischief. "Okay, fine. Meet me here." She pointed to the spot where she was standing.

I looked around the empty hallway dubiously. "Won't this place be locked up by then?"

Her smile was slow and mysterious as she held her hands up and wiggled her fingers like she was performing a magic trick. "I have my ways."

EIGHT

COLLETTE

I needed to breathe. That was all. Just breathe. In and out. In and o—

Holy mother of crap. What was I doing? Why was I standing in the shadows by the front door, waiting for Ethan to show up? *Was* he going to show up? Had I been duped?

I could see Bianca and Ethan now, sitting in his truck, watching me through a security camera. They were laughing and clinking glasses as they celebrated their evil plan to torture me.

Ugh.

I should have known better than to think Ethan was serious. Served me right for actually thinking I might have a chance with that Juilliard audition. This was why daydreams should be avoided at all costs—they inevitably led to disappointment. There would be no private dance sessions with Ethan, no miraculous opportunities to perform for the Juilliard scouts, and no swoon-worthy moments where Ethan-the-hottie-quarterback decided he wanted to kiss me.

Not that I'd been daydreaming about that or anything.

"Idiot," I mumbled as I stepped out of the shadows and moved to walk up the stairs. Thankfully, Mom had been so distracted after her meeting with the board that when we got home, she took a bottle of wine—that she still thinks I don't know is there—and barricaded herself in the room.

I knew I should have asked her if everything was all right, but I knew she would never tell me. And on the off chance that this was the first time she decided that her daughter was actually intelligent and a good listener, I didn't want to be late meeting Ethan.

It was disarming, this feeling of betrayal mixed with excitement. I felt like a rebel. Which was laughable. I'd never done anything that wasn't straight-laced and perfect—well, unless it dealt with me dancing alone.

Clandestine pirouettes might have been awkward to explain, but I wasn't exactly breaking the law. However, sneaking a boy into our all-girls' school after hours...?

That was another story altogether.

Just as I reached the top step, three solid knocks sounded on the door. I paused as excitement rushed through me. And then slowly, as if I were worried Ethan would somehow disappear if I moved too fast, I glanced toward the door.

When Ethan met my gaze, he lifted his hand and waved. I couldn't fight the smile that emerged on my lips. I nodded and then bounded down the stairs. I crossed the small foyer and then pressed on the metal bar to release the door.

"Hey," he said, as he stepped forward and entered.

I tried to ignore the fact that doing so brought him right next to me. His chest brushed against my arm, sending tingles racing across my skin. Had he meant to do that? Or was it just a coincidence?

Or was I overthinking this?

Yeah, I was definitely overthinking it.

I took a deep breath as I tried to calm my fluttering heart. I needed to remove all thoughts about Ethan and me being more than practice buddies. Because if I was reading this wrong—and I probably was—I didn't want to make a fool of myself. I doubt that I could come back from that.

Once he was inside the building, I let the door shut slowly behind me. Even though we were the only ones in the building, I didn't want to alert anyone walking by.

Ethan was carrying his guitar with him. I eyed it and then glanced up at him. He quirked an eyebrow and shrugged. "What?"

"So, it's just true." I shook my head as I walked in front of him and back up the stairs. "You really do play the guitar. I mean, I figured it was true but now that I see it, I know for sure."

He snorted so I looked over my shoulder at him. I was on the top step so I waited for him to join me.

"You thought I was lying about playing the guitar?"

I shrugged. "I don't know. Don't guys do stuff like that to make themselves sound cool?" Heat permeated my cheeks. I was telling myself to shut up, but my mouth wasn't listening. Apparently, I stunk at any type of flirting. I blamed my mother and this dumb, all-girls school.

"I'm the mayor's son and quarterback of the football team. I'm not sure having 'plays guitar' on my resume adds much."

I led him down the hallway to the only studio with its lights on. "Wow, humble much?" I teased.

His face reddened as he set his guitar down and turned. "I didn't mean...what I meant to say..."

I quirked my head to the side and then laughed. "I'm joking, Ethan. You've got a great...what did you call it? *Resume?* I'm sure there aren't many girls at Oakwood that would say no to you." My throat went dry as I realized what I was implying. Why couldn't I just stop talking?

Ethan had a smug look on his face as he studied me. "Was that...a compliment?"

I shrugged and turned, making my way over to the window where the stereo was sitting. I fiddled around with it, not sure what I was planning on doing. All I knew was I needed distance between us. It was scary, opening myself up to him like this. I always became second best to every guy in my life. Just ask my dad. He wrote the book *How to be a Deadbeat Dad*.

And for some reason, I didn't want the same ending with Ethan. I didn't want to be second place. I wasn't sure if I could handle that. The disappointment would lay a crushing blow.

"Hey, did I say something wrong?" Ethan's voice sounded from behind me. *Right* behind me.

I yelped and turned to see that his eyes were wide. He raised his hands as if to surrender. I pressed my hand to my heart and blew out my breath. "Geez. Don't sneak up on me like that."

He smiled. His goofy smile that made my knees turn weak. "I could add ninja to my resume."

I laughed. Out loud and unabashed. The light in Ethan's eyes grew brighter. Like a kid on Christmas morning. Did that mean what I wanted it to mean? Did he like talking to me? Making me laugh?

Before I basked in the warmth that was talking and flirting with Ethan, I cleared my throat and walked over to the wall where I grabbed a chair. "You're going first," I said.

It was almost like a rain cloud had suddenly appeared over Ethan. He furrowed his brow as he dropped his gaze. "I was hoping we would dance first."

I shook my head. "Nope. You've already seen mine, now it's time I see yours." I nodded toward his guitar case.

A sinister expression passed over Ethan's face and I had to sigh and roll my eyes. I knew he would take what I said the wrong way the moment it left my lips. "That's not what I meant," I said as I dragged the chair into the center of the studio.

Ethan shrugged as he followed me. "I didn't say anything."

I turned and narrowed my eyes as I placed my hands on my hips. "Yeah, but I know what you were thinking."

Ethan leaned into me, not at all threatened by my five-foot-five frame. He towered over me and I had to say, I liked it. Maybe a little too much.

"I highly doubt you know what I'm thinking," he said.

I wasn't sure, but I could have sworn his voice had deepened. And there was this look in his eyes. This mysterious, sexy, bad boy look that had my heart galloping in my chest. My breath had turned heavy and my body tingled as my thoughts started racing.

"I think I do." My voice had turned breathy. Well, if my on-fire body hadn't been a dead giveaway to him, my dumb voice was a homing beacon to him. Suddenly, my cool collected manner had been replaced by a bright red blinking light that said 'come on over here, Collette is attracted to you.'

He leaned closer and I couldn't help but notice how that movement brought his lips inches from mine. I could smell his cologne. He smelled of sandalwood and cinnamon. And his body? It was like standing next to a heated blanket. For a split second, I wondered what it would feel like to be wrapped up next to him—and then I pushed that ridiculous thought from my mind.

I needed to get my head on straight. Right now.

I took a step back and waved my hand to the chair. "You're

worried I'm going to laugh," I said, forcing my voice to return to normal and my snarky smile to spread across my lips.

Ethan blinked a few times, like he hadn't expected me to step away or speak. His brows furrowed as he met my gaze. Then, recognition passed over his face and he snorted. "I wasn't thinking that," he said as he winked. Winked!

Great. Now all of the control I'd had over my thoughts were balled up and tossed out the window. *What did a wink mean?*

"But I am now," he said as he sat down on the chair and then lifted his hand and waved his fingers. "Bring me my guitar," he commanded.

I thought about making a comment about how I wasn't his servant, but then held my tongue. We'd already done enough flirting this evening, I feared I would explode if I did anymore.

Besides, I needed to prepare myself for what was coming after the guitar playing. Ethan was literally going to have his hands all over me. Touching me. Bringing my body close to his.

My heart started thumping in my chest as I reached down and picked up his guitar case. There were those two conflicting emotions again. Fear and excitement made my body feel numb. I knew how to process one on its own, but together? They made my head feel foggy and my body light.

This must be what it's like to skydive.

Luckily, once I handed Ethan's guitar over to him, his playful demeanor changed. A sort of stoic expression fell on his face as he set the guitar case down on the ground and unclipped the latches. Then he opened it, revealing a dark wood acoustic guitar.

I'd never seen someone have so much reverence for an instrument before. The way he held it, tuned it. It was like the guitar was a part of him that had finally come home.

It was how I felt about ballet.

All witty comebacks flew from my mind and all I could do was settle down on the floor a few feet away from him and watch. He strummed a few notes and then shook his head as he stopped and fiddled with the tuning keys. Then he would resituate himself and strum again.

About ten minutes passed before he settled into his seat and raised his gaze up to meet mine. There was this shy, worried look there that caused my breath to catch in my throat.

"Are you ready?" he asked, again with a wink.

What was with all the winking? Was this new or had he always been a winker?

I cleared my throat. "For what?"

He strummed loudly and quickly as he raised his eyebrows. Then he stopped and raised his hand up in an exaggerated way. "To be *blown away*."

I rolled my eyes as I brought my legs up to hug them. Then I faked a yawn. "Eh, we'll see."

Ethan got a determined look on his face and turned his focus to his guitar. Music filled the studio and he closed his eyes. The sound, the beat, it all flowed through me in a way I'd never had happen before.

And then, when he parted his lips and began to sing, my life slowed down. It sounds dumb to say that time moved in slow motion, but it did. All I could see, all I wanted to see, was Ethan.

His voice was deep and rich as the words left his lips. His expression moved with the song like he was living it as he created it. He was a different person. He looked whole. He looked...happy.

Once the song ended, he let the last few notes hang in the air before he clutched the neck of the guitar and turned his attention to me. I'm not sure what I looked like, but it must have been unnerving because his brow furrowed and a worried look passed through his gaze.

He cleared his throat and raised his eyebrows. "So, yeah, that's me playing the guitar."

Not sure how to express the emotions that he evoked in me, I did the only thing that came to mind. I clapped.

Ethan stared at me as I rose to my feet. "Ethan, you're amazing," I said as my clap died down.

He narrowed his eyes and blew out his breath. "You're just saying that," he said. For a fleeting moment, I saw a small smile tug on the corners of his lips.

I had no problem telling someone when they did great. And Ethan *was* amazing. "I have to admit, I was skeptical. But now that I've witnessed it, you've got to pursue this. It's not just a hobby."

He studied me for a moment before he dropped his gaze. "Yeah, well, my dad will never go for it." He sighed as he strummed a few chords. "You know, family legacy and all."

I did know. I knew what it was like to disappoint and it sucked. If I could meet the requirements of dancing, I was pretty sure I would do it even if I hated it. I was desperate for my mother's approval. Because when it's gone, it sucks.

"Does he know?" I asked.

Ethan glanced up at me. "Does your mom know?"

Heat pricked at the back of my neck. "It's different for me," I said as I turned. I didn't want Ethan to see the pain that was so close to the surface. Blast him and his emotional songs that had me all out of whack.

"I'm sorry," he said in a tone that told me that he was being honest.

I glanced over at him to see that his shoulders were slumped. He smiled at me when I caught his eye.

"Seems like this is a touchy subject for both of us." He

strummed a few times. "I guess having your dreams on display is always hard."

I swallowed, forcing down all of the emotions that felt lodged there and nodded. "Yeah."

He started on another song and I wandered over to the window and glanced out. The sun was setting, causing oranges and purples to streak the sky. I wrapped my arms around my chest and let out a breath.

Normally, I kept things bottled up. But the fact that he felt the same for playing the guitar as I did for dancing changed things.

It was like he knew what I was going through. The desires and disappointments that came from wanting something in direct contrast to what your parents wanted.

I tightened my arms. My heart hurt and for some reason, holding my arms closer to my chest felt like a way to suppress that hurt.

I knew what Ethan and I were doing was temporary. There was no way we could keep this up forever. At some point, his father was going to realize that he was amazing and accept Ethan as a musician. Then Ethan would go off, become the next guitar playing president.

He could change his future if he wanted to. I was sure of it. There was nothing inherently wrong with him that would stop him from him pursuing his dreams. But me?

I wasn't going to be able to change. No matter how much I wished or tried, some things weren't in the cards for me. And where would I be then?

Right where I was in this moment.

My future wasn't going to change and right now, that was hurting me more than ever.

His voice behind me drew me out of my thoughts.

"Ethan is walking toward you now," he said in a comically low voice, like a broadcaster or a narrator or something.

I whipped around to face him. "What are you doing?"

"I'm announcing my presence," he said matter-of-factly. "Didn't want to sneak up on you again. Although..." One of his eyebrows hitched up as he stopped in front of me. "You *are* pretty cute when you're scared."

He gave me a smile that was magic—it had to be magic. What other explanation could there be for the way that smile made my heart stop hurting?

"I wasn't *scared*." That was what I said aloud. In my head, a voice was screaming, *He thinks I'm cute?*

"Uh huh," he said. "Whatever you say."

He was teasing. Maybe even flirting. And I...I *loved* it.

Thoughts of the future and my mother—they didn't stand a chance when he was looking at me like this, with his eyes full of laughter and his lips curving up in a sexy smile that seemed like it was meant just for me.

"You're up next," he said, nodding toward the dance floor.

I blinked as nerves hit me like a bucket of ice water. I wasn't nervous about the dancing—that I could do in my sleep. It was the fact that he'd be seeing me in my leotard again, and that he'd be *touching me*.

"Come on," he said as he set his guitar back in the case. "What are you so worried about? I've already seen you dance, remember? I already know that you're amazing."

A tremulous smile tugged at my lips despite this new, crippling fear. "Amazing, huh?"

He grinned, and moved closer. "Show me what you need me to do."

My throat worked as I tried to swallow past the nerves and the fear that was creeping up my insides making it hard to speak. But he was waiting for me, and it was now or never.

I didn't think; I just acted. Grabbing his hands and placing them on my waist. They were large and warm, and the feel of his hands on me made my heart leap in my chest.

I looked up, bracing myself for his reaction as he felt my softness. But all I saw there in his eyes was warmth.

Heat, actually.

His brown eyes were darker than ever as they met mine. "What now?"

Had his voice always been this low and rumbly? I could feel it, like a bass line thrumming through me. I swallowed again, and this time my throat worked. I drew in a deep breath. "You won't be lifting me today," I said, trying to keep my tone matter-of-fact. "I don't want to injure Oakwood's star quarterback."

He laughed and his hands tightened on my waist. "I can handle it."

I can't.

I cleared my throat. "Maybe. But there's more involved than just picking me up," I said. "Male ballet dancers aren't just brutes who're good at heavy lifting. There are movements you need to learn first."

His smile widened with amusement. "Did you just call me a brute?"

I gave a huff of laughter. His teasing was helping to put me at ease, and I was starting to get comfortable with him touching me, especially since he hadn't run away in horror.

"I meant it in the nicest possible way," I said, donning a sugary sweet smile that made him laugh again.

"Well, okay then." He leaned down slightly so his face was close to mine. "Tell me what you want me to do."

Kiss me. Touch me. Tell me you think I'm pretty.

Oh, the thoughts that went through my head were dangerous. And ridiculous. But the nerves were gone now, and I was filled with that crazy sense of freedom that comes with conquering a fear.

Maybe it was adrenaline, I don't know. All I did know was that I was ready to dance, and for the first time in my life?

I had a partner.

NINE

ETHAN

The next two weeks were almost too good to be true. I'd finally found a place to play whatever I wanted for as long as I wanted. And I'd also found the world's best audience. And the fact that the audience was as cute and snarky as Collette only made my new normal that much better.

I sat in the studio with Collette one afternoon, trying to still my nerves. I could feel Collette's gaze on me. Why I thought playing her a new song I'd been playing around with was a good idea, I'd never know. She was going to hate what I did. I was sure of it.

The sounds of my last chord still lingered in the air when I lifted my head. "So?" I asked. "What do you think?"

She was sitting on the ground before me, leaning against the floor-to-ceiling mirror, her legs stretched out before her. Her expression was thoughtful and slightly dazed.

I loved this look. It was the look she got every time I played for her, like she was lost to the music, her mind somewhere else. Somewhere beautiful.

I would have given anything to know what she was thinking about when I played.

She tilted her head to the side like she was considering my question. This was another thing I loved about our 'private sessions,' as we'd started calling them. When it came to music and dance, she never gave flippant answers. She was snarky and sarcastic about almost everything else, but when it came to the arts, she was totally sincere.

"I liked it," she said slowly. "I love the way you slowed it down and made it your own. I've heard that song a million times on the radio and never realized the melody was so beautiful."

My chest swelled with happiness at the compliment and I had to smother a goofy grin. "Thanks."

She shifted, coming to her feet. "I think my favorite is still the Coldplay song. Will you play that one next?"

"Sure." I knew which one she meant. *Fix You.* I'd played that for her the second time we'd met up and I'd looked up from my guitar to find her sitting there with tears in her eyes. I kept my head down as I strummed the first few notes.

I wouldn't be able to make it through to the end of the song if I saw her cry again. Seeing her sad had nearly killed me, and it had taken everything in me not to pull her into my arms.

In fact, it was getting harder and harder not to hold her, touch her...kiss her like I wanted to. Touching her while dancing was one thing. Showing her how I had begun to feel was something completely different.

My fingers fumbled on the strings and I shoved that thought away.

This was our fourth private session over the last two weeks, and each one had been better than the last. It seemed, the more comfortable we were with each other, the better we were able to perform.

But it was a catch-22. The more I was with her, the more relaxed I'd become which made it harder to keep from acting on these pesky feelings that had decided to show up and not leave me alone. I wanted to kiss her. There was no doubt in my mind about that—but I was pretty sure I'd missed my moment. Like, back when we'd first met maybe I could have gotten away with that—I could have laughed it off if she'd rejected me. I could have just apologized for misreading the situation and moved on. But now?

Now we were *friends*.

And I was pretty sure my current address was the friend zone.

I lifted my head as I started to sing the chorus—badly, no doubt, since it was way too high for me—and then I stopped.

She was dancing. To my music.

And she was stunning.

My heart seemed to trip over itself like it was trying to keep pace with her rapid footwork. Luckily, I knew this song by heart because my fingers plucked the strings by rote as I watched her move.

So graceful. Her body was perfection, and it was made to dance.

I didn't know how she didn't see that. More importantly, I couldn't fathom how her mother didn't see it. Collette was liquid energy, all flowing movements and supple grace.

My mouth was dry and my heart was hammering...I couldn't look away from her, not even when the final chord had long since died off, leaving us in silence.

She'd come to a stop with her back to me.

"That was beautiful," I said, hoping she could hear my sincerity. Hoping she could hear everything I couldn't bring myself to say.

"I was just goofing off." Her voice was little more than a

murmur. Like she was embarrassed or something. Which was irritating. I hated that she was so humble. It was getting annoying.

I'd never seen her move like that before. Like she was a part of the music, or the music was inside of her. It had been a thing of beauty, and I was blown away because...because I'd been a part of it. My music and her dancing had been intertwined, making something that was bigger than both of us, and that? That was mind blowing.

"Was that your own choreography?" I just wanted her to turn, to talk to me, to tell me that she felt it too. I wanted to see her eyes. Feel her stare on my face. It had been real and I wanted to share it with her on a deeper level.

"No," she said, her voice louder than before as she reached for a hoodie. "That was Coldplay's choreography." She turned toward me with a smirk. "Chris Martin does that every night on stage."

"Funny," I said. But I let it drop. Her sarcasm would have been a dead giveaway that she was uncomfortable with my praise, even if her cheeks weren't turning pink. I couldn't understand why she never just took the praise. I meant it. All of it.

"So," she said, her tone brisk. "When are you going to play your own songs for me?"

I let out an exasperated huff of amusement. "I told you. Ryan's the songwriter." I shrugged. "I just like to play."

She leaned against the mirror as she studied me. "Okay then, when am I going to hear Ryan's songs?"

I stood up, holding my guitar by its neck as I walked toward her and the case that was right next to her. My heart was beating so hard I could hear it. "Yeah, well..." I took a deep breath. "I actually wanted to talk to you about that."

She tilted her head to the side and wrapped the hoodie

around herself in a now-familiar gesture. I thought about saying something, but then fought the urge. I'd said things before and she just laughed it off. It was frustrating, the fact that my thoughts were brushed off so quickly. But I was learning with Collette, she didn't like to be pushed and I could respect that. For now.

I decided to focus on laying my guitar down in its case.

I cleared my throat, trying not to overthink what I was about to talk to her about. I mean, she'd heard me play a million times now, seeing me on stage wasn't that big a deal. It wasn't like I was asking her on a real date or anything. "Ryan's band is performing at The Tailgate next week. Thursday night, actually."

She watched me steadily. "Oh yeah?"

"Yeah, and, uh...his guitarist can't make it. He's going to be out of town with his family, so, um..." I swallowed. Crap, why was this so hard to spit out. "So I'm going to stand in for him."

Her smile was slow and brilliant. "That's awesome, Ethan."

"Yeah, thanks." Just spit it out. "I was wondering if maybe you'd want to go. And you know...watch."

I wouldn't have thought it was possible for her smile to get any bigger. But it was. And it did.

She shocked the life out of me by dropping her arms and launching toward me to give me a hug.

I stood frozen for a second as her arms wrapped around my waist. I looked down at the top of her head in stunned silence as she squeezed me tight. I shook off the shock and wrapped my arms around her too, returning the hug.

"I am so excited for you," she gushed, her face pressed against my shoulder and her hair tickling my nose. I tried not to notice the feel of her curves pressed against me, or how good she felt in my arms. I'd held her countless times now as part of her dance routine, but never like this.

She pulled back slightly to look up at me. "And I'm so glad you finally told me."

I blinked stupidly as her words registered. It wasn't until she took a step back that I was able to form words. "You *knew?*"

She gave me an impish grin. "Tilly might have said something."

I arched my brows in question. Tilly was the dancer assigned to help Ryan catch up on the basics of ballet, but I wasn't sure how she knew anything about our upcoming gig.

"I guess Ryan bragged to Tilly about the concert and how you were stepping in." She shifted, waving a hand in the air like the rest was obvious. "She told Eve and Eve told me and..." She sighed. "You know how ballerinas are. They're the worst gossips."

I shook my head. "I didn't know that, actually, but, uh... why didn't you say anything?"

She shrugged. "I figured if you wanted me to know, you'd tell me."

"So?" I asked. "Will you come?"

"Of course!"

Any flicker of hope I might have felt that maybe this would be our first date was killed quick when she smacked my shoulder in a decidedly friendly manner. "I wouldn't miss my practice buddy's big debut."

I forced a smile. Practice buddy. Right.

Awesome.

"Will your mom be cool with it?" I asked.

"If I tell her it's an outing that involves the great Ethan Morrison?" She arched her brows. "She'll probably offer to drive me herself."

I grinned. It had become something of a joke between us, how much her mom loved me. Not that I was such a great dancer or anything—I definitely wasn't. But once her mom got wind that I was the mayor's son? The term 'teacher's pet' may or may not have become my new nickname in class.

"You're not really going to tell her though, right?" I winced because I knew the answer but I still had to ask.

She rolled her eyes. "No, of course not." She dropped her voice two octaves and donned a terrible mob boss voice as she added, "I keep your secrets, you keep mine, right?"

I laughed as I shook my head. "You're ridiculous."

She laughed too as she smacked my arm again like I was her brother. "And you're an idiot if you think I'd out your secret just to get a ride. I'll figure out something to tell my mom."

I nodded, trying to play it cool, trying not to show how relieved I was that she'd agreed to go, or how excited I was, or how crazy nervous.

"What are you going to tell your parents?" she asked.

That...was a good question. "I haven't figured that out yet."

She gave me a sympathetic look as she nodded.

She now knew better than anyone what my situation was like at home. Thanks to Coach Reynolds talking to my dad, he was now on board with me taking ballet classes. The fact that he hadn't listened to me, but had listened to my coach?

That was the reason I didn't feel guilty lying to him and my mom about where I was when I was practicing with Collette. Dance practice ran long, coach made me take an extra class this week—he thinks it's helping my throw...

I was getting good at lying. Not exactly something I was proud of, but for the first time in my life I was doing something for myself and not for others, and it felt freakin' amazing.

There was just one more thing that I wanted—something far more complicated than time to play guitar. And she was standing right in front of me right now, grinning like a clown. I shoved my hands in my pockets as my heart rate picked up speed. "So, about Thursday," I started slowly. "Maybe after the show—"

The studio door slammed open and I jerked back as Collette whipped around.

"Oh!" A short, black-haired Latina girl was standing in the doorway staring at me, her eyes wide with shock and her mouth hanging open.

For a heartbeat we all just stood there, stunned.

The black-haired girl snapped out of it first. "I'm so sorry," she said, her gaze moving from me to Collette as she grimaced. "I am so, so sorry. I didn't mean to interrupt." She shook her head, her curls bouncing from the movement.

She was starting to walk out and pull the door shut behind her but Collette stopped her. "Olivia, wait," she said. "Get back in here."

Olivia turned back around and came in, a guilty expression on her face. But that didn't stop her from eyeing me like I was some animal at the zoo.

"Olivia, this is Ethan," Collette said.

Olivia's eyes narrowed on me. "Ethan," she repeated. She turned to Collette and muttered something that sounded like, "Graceful, unique, and beautiful?"

Collette blushed as she ignored her friend and turned to me. "Ethan, this is my friend Olivia."

"Nice to meet—"

"What are you doing here?" Collette asked, her voice sounded strained as she turned back to her friend.

Olivia was wearing a smug little smile as she crossed her arms. "I was going to watch Dancing with the Stars and I thought you might want to join me. I figured you might be down here, but—" Her gaze darted over to me. "I had no idea you were doing your own version down here." My skin heated as Olivia's gaze dropped down to my spats. They weren't something I normally wore but I was tired of hearing Collette complain about the lack of movement my sweatpants created.

"We were just..." Collette's eyes widened as she looked at me, like she wasn't sure how to finish that sentence.

"We were rehearsing," I said.

Olivia frowned. "For what?" Then, before either of us could respond, she whipped her head around to face Collette. "Wait a second, did you decide to audition for Juilliard?"

"What?" Collette's voice was a squeak and her face turned a deep shade of red. "No, of course not."

"Juilliard," I repeated, trying to make sense of this conversation.

Collette turned to me, and I knew I wasn't imagining that panicky look in her eyes. "Yeah, it's a school for dance and music, and it's super prestigious—"

"I know what Juilliard is," I said.

"Right, well, you never know," she said. "I figured it they don't have a football team, you wouldn't have heard of it."

I frowned at her in confusion. She looked flustered, and she wouldn't quite make eye contact. Not to mention, she was treating me like some dumb jock and not the guy she'd been discussing music and dance with for the past two weeks.

"They have scouts coming in two weeks," Olivia explained.

"Yeah, I've heard some of the girls talking about it in class," I said. But Collette hadn't mentioned it, and I'd figured that was because she hadn't been invited to audition. From what Bianca and the others said, it was a big deal to be invited, and only the top girls in the academy had been picked. I turned to her. "Is that what you've been rehearsing for?"

"No, of course not." Her tone was off, her body on edge. After weeks of watching this girl dance, I knew how she moved, which meant I knew her tells.

"Do you want to audition?" I asked.

She met my gaze evenly as she repeated herself. "No, of course not."

"You're lying." I never looked away from Collette but I was vaguely aware of Olivia watching us intently, her head swiveling back and forth like this was a tennis match.

Collette pursed her lips, her brows drawing down in a scowl as she faced off with me. After a long moment, she let out a harsh exhale. "Okay, fine. I'd love to audition. But it's never going to happen." She arched her brows and widened her eyes in an expression that said *are you happy now?*

I wasn't. Not even a tiny bit. But I also didn't want to have this conversation in front of Olivia. She might have been Collette's friend, but I didn't know her. What I had to say to Collette needed to be said in private.

She seemed to sense that I was giving up this battle—temporarily, at least—and she burst into motion, gathering up her bookbag and her water bottle. "So, when do you want to practice again?"

It was a not-so-subtle hint that our current practice session was now over.

She glanced over her shoulder at me. "Tomorrow?"

I shook my head. "I've got a game tomorrow."

"Oh. Right." She gave her head a little shake. "I forgot."

"Actually..." I grabbed my guitar case and came over to her. "I was wondering if maybe you wanted to come."

She blinked up at me. "Where?"

Olivia gave a little snort near the door but we both ignored her.

"To the game."

Collette's eyes widened in surprise as I fidgeted with the case in my hands. "I, uh...I mean..."

"She'd love to go," Olivia said. We both turned to look at her and she grinned. "Isn't that right, Collette?"

Collette nodded, turning back to me with a little smile of her own. "Yeah. Sure. I'd love to go."

I grinned as I backed away toward the door. A date it was not. It wasn't even close since I'd be on the field all night.

But it was something.

TEN

COLLETTE

I sat in my car outside the academy's dorm entrance, tapping my fingers on the steering wheel as I waited for Olivia to come out. I couldn't believe she'd gotten me into this...and now she was making us late.

We were supposed to be on our way to Ethan's football game and yet, I felt like I was on my way to the dentist. It was going to be painful, I just knew it.

Which was why I'd tried to cancel on Olivia all day at school today only to have her sigh and look me in the eye as she told me to stop being a wuss.

I finally groaned and told her if I had to go, then I was driving so I could decide when we left. She'd squealed and hugged me. And now here I sat, waiting. I'd texted her about ten times only to get a thumbs-up emoji as a response. It was hard, sitting here, waiting for my best friend to finish beautifying herself. Not that I could blame her. After all, we went to a school with absolutely no boys. It wasn't a wonder why she was taking her time.

I was about to turn my car off and climb out to hurry her

along, but the door opened and she stepped out—in a mini skirt and a tank top. Half of her hair was pulled up onto the top of her head in a messy bun.

She smiled and waved as she hurried over.

I glanced down at my dark red hoodie and jeans and blew out my breath. *I wasn't going to be jealous. I wasn't going to be jealous.* I needed to keep chanting that in my mind because the green monster was starting to awaken inside of me.

Which just made me feel worse. What kind of friend was I? I couldn't be happy for Olivia when I felt bad about myself. But I couldn't feel good about myself, especially when I was around my practically perfect best friend. It was a vicious cycle.

The passenger door flew open and Olivia dropped down onto the seat. She grinned at me as she reached up and grabbed her seatbelt. "Sorry," she said sheepishly. The click of the buckle sounded in the silence as I pulled away from the curb.

"It's okay," I said. I swallowed a few times and felt my irritation with my situation lessen. It wasn't Olivia's fault and she shouldn't suffer because of my issues.

After all, if I let it bother me, that made me a pretty crappy friend.

"So, tell me more about Ethan."

I paused at the stoplight and glanced over at her. She was grinning like a fool as she studied me. I shook my head and pressed on the gas as soon as the light turned green.

"Oh, no. We are not going to go there. Ethan is just a friend. That is all." I was grateful that I sounded more confident than I felt. My feelings for Ethan were beginning to change and I was one hundred percent sure those changes were felt only on my end.

Ethan was the unsuspecting guy that I was finding myself falling for. But how could I not? After all, he was exactly what I didn't know I wanted in a guy. He was sweet. Funny. Sexy. Gosh, that boy. He lifted me like I weighed nothing and when he wrapped his arms around me?

I felt small and protected.

I never knew I could feel like that.

Olivia snorted and my cheeks flushed. Crap. I had told myself to stop thinking of Ethan like that and yet, here I was breaking my own rule.

"What?" I said as I tucked my hair behind my ear.

"Nothing." Then Olivia leaned over. "You're just blushing and you got this goofy look on your face. I have a feeling that a certain brooding football player may be the source of that reaction." Then she raised her hands and made air quotes as she said, "But you're 'just friends' so what do I know?"

I tightened my grip on the steering wheel as I calmed the butterflies in my stomach. "We *are* just friends."

"Uh huh."

I glared at her. "We are."

"Mmhmm."

"Olivia," I groaned as I turned on my blinker and merged into the lane next to us. We were a few streets away from Oakwood High and I needed her to believe me before we climbed out of the car. I couldn't have my friend ruining what I had with Ethan.

She was sweet but she was about as subtle as a bomb.

Olivia must have picked up on my desperation because she nodded and held up her hands. "Okay, fine. You're just friends."

Relief coursed through my veins as I glanced over at her. She was snapping her gum and staring out the window. "Does he have any single friends? You know, for someone who doesn't want to be *just friends* with a hot football player?"

I cleared my throat and shrugged. "There are a few guys on

his team that I think are single. One is Ryan and the other is Cooper. They're both cute."

Olivia smiled over at me. "Okay, okay. I can get on board with that. Can you ask him to introduce me?"

I shrugged as I pulled into the parking lot, narrowly missing an overly supportive parent who sprinted past. He was completely decked out in hunter green and silver attire. Another parent appeared in similar garb and they both high fived before they disappeared between the parked cars.

"It's like some weird social experiment here," Olivia said, craning her neck for a better look at a mom hoisting signs that said "We're #1!"

"Sports parents are different than ballet parents," I said as I pulled into an empty parking spot and turned off the engine. The type of parents surrounding us was only the tip of the iceberg. The students who were flocking into the stadium were just as strange. To us, at least. For a second, I wondered what my life would be like if I'd gone to a normal school with normal kids. If I'd grown up with boys in my life and surrounded by people of all shapes and sizes...

But I hadn't. And watching a horde of teen guys walk past my car with their, all their booming voices and indecipherable shouts made me feel like a stranger in a strange land. I was fighting the urge to slip my key back into the ignition and get the heck out of here. This was so not my scene.

I knew how to be around Ethan when he and I were in the studio but out in public? How was I supposed to act?

We weren't boyfriend and girlfriend, and besides Olivia, no one else knew that we spent time together. I'd say we were friends, but even that didn't feel right. Friends didn't have clandestine rendezvous after dark, now did they?

We were secret...somethings.

How do secret somethings act in public?

"Relax," Olivia said.

I glanced over at her. Her eyebrows were furrowed as she studied me. Then she smiled. "He invited you, remember? He's going to be so excited that you're here."

I swallowed as I nodded but didn't move to get out. I took in a deep breath and turned to look at Olivia. "How do I act? I mean, we have fun in the studio but this is the first time we are doing anything together...in public."

Olivia chewed her gum with a thoughtful expression before she reached out and rested her hand on mine. "It's just a football game. I'm guessing he's going to spend most of his time on the field throwing a ball around." A smile spread across her lips as she held my gaze. "But I could be wrong."

I sighed and rolled my eyes. "Well, duh."

Olivia chuckled as she climbed out of the car. "Other than that, just let him lead. From what I can see, he likes you."

I raised my eyebrows. That word *likes* had so many meanings to it and I wanted to know which one she meant.

She sighed. "I only saw the two of you together for, like, a few minutes so I can't confirm or deny, but from what I *did* see, he didn't seem repulsed by you. And he was pretty insistent that you come to his game."

We slammed our doors at the same time and Olivia waited for me as I made my way around the car. Then we fell into step with each other as we headed to the ticket booth.

"From my experience, guys don't just invite random girls places. So I'd take it as a good sign that he wants to see more of you."

I stared at the ground as we walked across the parking lot. On one hand, I didn't want my best friend to lie to me. But on the other hand...I desperately wished she'd lie to me. I wanted her to tell me a big old whopper about how it'd been so crazy obvious that he was into me. One second in the same room and she'd been overwhelmed by all the sexual tension.

But Olivia didn't lie, and I was left trying to figure out if the phrase 'he didn't seem repulsed by you' was something to cheer about. "So, I should think he at least tolerates me?" I peeked over at Olivia.

"He probably more than tolerates you, but I can't say for sure. Not when you'd pretty much kept this *huge part of your life a secret from your best friend.*"

She sort of yelled that last part and I shot her an apologetic look. She just laughed. "It's okay. I already told you, I forgive you."

We were standing at the window now. An older woman wearing a shirt that said "Football Mom: This Beauty raised her Beast." She had a green and silver hat on complete with black streaks across her cheeks.

I raised my eyebrows, trying to imagine my mother doing something similar in support of me, but couldn't picture it. The woman behind the counter didn't seem to notice that I was staring. Instead, she handed me two tickets and I handed her a twenty.

"Man, I wish our parents were this supportive about dancing," Olivia said as I handed her the second ticket and we fell into line to enter the stadium.

"I was just thinking that. You'd think for artsy people, they could at least come with a sign or something." I nodded toward the group of giggling girls that were holding a sign that said "Run, run, number twenty-one."

"Yeah. You'd think," Olivia said.

We handed our tickets to the guard. He took them, ripped them, and then waved us through.

Once we got through the gates, the chaos didn't end. Parents, siblings, and other Oakwood students were all running and weaving through each other as they either stood in line for concessions or tried to push through to get seats.

Olivia and I got a container of nachos to split and two waters. Then we started up the stadium stairs to find a seat. It was crowded but we found two empty seats between a group of teen guys and a family. Lucky me, I got stuck sitting next to one of the too-loud boys who'd never learned the meaning of 'personal space.'

As soon as I got situated, my phone chimed. I handed my water to Olivia to hold and pulled my phone from my hoodie pocket.

Ethan

My heart pounded as I swiped my phone on and read his text.

Ethan: I think I see you. You're the only person crazy enough to wear a hoodie in seventy degree weather.

My cheeks heated as I glanced around. When I didn't see him, I furrowed my brow.

Me: Where are you?

"Who are you texting?" Olivia asked as she craned her neck to look at my screen.

I tipped my phone toward my chest and shook my head. "No one," I lied, knowing full well that my reaction to his text was most likely giving me away.

Olivia rolled her eyes. "Yeah, okay." Then she nudged me with her shoulder. "Please tell him that I expect him to introduce me to some eligible guy." She dipped a chip into the cheese and then stuck the whole thing in her mouth.

My phone chimed again. Thankfully Olivia was engrossed with eating so I took what time I had to look at his message.

Ethan: I have eyes everywhere

Me: Okay now that's just creepy

I got a clown face emoji in response. Laughing under my breath, I started to type more but he beat me to it.

Ethan: Hey, did you know you're wearing our rival's colors? Try not to get into any fights up there.

I looked down at the sidelines but it was packed with marching band members and cheerleaders. I spotted some jerseys too, but not Ethan's dark hair or familiar build.

The guys next to me were laughing over something and then they were pushing and shoving and...yours truly got an elbow in the shoulder.

"Oh man, sorry," the blond next to me said.

"No biggie." I forced a smile.

His friend shoved him again and I was unceremoniously bumped again.

"Yo, cut it out," blond guy shouted at his friends.

He gave me another apologetic wince. "Sorry, my friends are idiots."

The last shoving contest had spilled the guy's popcorn on the ground and I was leaning over to help him pick it up when my phone dinged again.

I focused back on my phone as soon as the guy beside me turned away. The eagerness to see what Ethan had written was making me feel ridiculously girly and giddy and...if I wasn't careful, I'd start getting *giggly*.

I never did giggly. I was so *not* a giggler.

Ethan: Are you here with someone?

I glanced over at Olivia who was still munching away before I texted back.

Me: Of course.

What, did he really think I'd come alone? I might not have been crazy popular, but I did have some friends, thank you very much.

Me: Speaking of...Do you have any single friends?

I waited. The three little dots kept appearing and disappearing. Finally, his message came through.

Ethan: Why?

Me: Because you have a single friend.

Ethan: (confused expression emoji) You're single? When were you dating someone?

I furrowed my brow and then burst out laughing. He thought that I was talking about me. And when I scrolled back up to see autocorrect had changed "I" to "you" I felt my cheeks flush. Great. Now he'd think I wanted him to set me up with one of his friends.

How freakin' mortifying. I scrambled to make things right.

Me: Ack! I meant I have a single friend. You. I didn't mean me.

Crap. What was wrong with me? I hadn't even been able to finish my text before I accidentally hit send.

Ethan: I'm single?

I stared at the phone, heat pulsating through my body with every beat of my crazy, spastic heart. Why did my phone hate me? Why did fate do this to me?

Me: Tried to type I again and instead my phone changed it to you. And then my big, fat thumb hit the send button before I could finish.

Three little dancing dots. I held my breath, waiting to see if I needed to fix this again, or if he understood what I was trying to say.

Ethan: Who needs a boyfriend?

I was making a mess of this. I contemplated spelling my current relationship status out for him but feared what my phone might do with it: might as well have spelled it out for him. *I am available. Super single. Never been kissed, in fact. Ask me out now, please and thank you.*

Ethan: So...you're not single?

Yup, I'd officially made a mess of this. He was probably really confused right now. Heck, I was confused right now. I stared at my phone, trying to think of a response that didn't make me sound pathetic or lame. With all the time we'd spent together, if I had a boyfriend, I would have mentioned it. He couldn't really think I had a boyfriend. I had no idea how to respond so in a fit of bravery I decided to try something terrifying.

I was going to flirt.

Me: I'm in hot demand, didn't you know? I've got men in every city.

I added a little winky face emoji and sent that text and then waited for a response.

Ethan: I believe it. I'd say you beat them off with a stick, but I've seen those legs of yours. You don't need a stick.

I swallowed as heat raced to my cheeks. There was a laughing emoji at the end. Was he making fun of me? Or was he just teasing? I couldn't tell and my first reaction was to assume the worst. After all, if that's what I thought about myself, it only made sense that others thought it too.

Not sure what to do and the band starting up, I slipped my phone back into the pocket of my hoodie and shoved my hands in as well. I didn't want to get upset but I couldn't help but fear what Ethan really thought.

Was I just fooling myself to think that he could really care about me like that? Or was I just a girl who had an empty studio for him to use? If that was the case, then he might as well date my mom for all I cared. I had access to the same things she did.

My phone chimed again, but I chose to ignore it. I didn't

want to hear what he had to say. I was used to other people making small jabs at my weight but I never expected it from him.

I was the idiot who'd begun to care for him.

Olivia was cheering as the team ran onto the field, followed by the cheerleaders. It was salt in the wound when I saw just how skinny and perky the cheerleaders were as they shook their pom poms and chanted something about being aggressive.

A rock had settled in my stomach as I wrapped my arms around my waist and leaned forward. I wanted to run home and hide in my room where Ethan couldn't hurt me. Juilliard couldn't hurt me. And I'd be alone, which was okay with me. I'd accepted that fate a long time ago.

I just needed to endure this game and then I'd be free.

These things only lasted like an hour, right? I could last an hour.

ELEVEN

ETHAN

Cooper's meaty hand came down on my shoulder like an anvil as he passed me on the way out of the lockers. "Good game, man."

"Thanks, Coop. You too," I said. It had been a good game. We'd not only won, we'd slaughtered the other team. I should have been ecstatic, laughing it up with the other guys but instead, I felt like I was going to lose my mind if I didn't find Collette soon and get some answers.

Ryan slid onto the bench seat next to me as he wrestled on his combat boots. "You coming out with us to celebrate?"

"I, uh..." I hope not. "I'm not sure yet."

I glanced down at my phone. Still nothing. My after-game plans were entirely dependent on a cute little brunette who still hadn't responded to my last text.

Do you have a boyfriend?

This should not have been a difficult question to answer. My gut churned as I realized that the fact that she hadn't answered...? That was probably my answer right there.

Idiot.

I was such an idiot. How had I never thought to ask her that before? I guess I'd just assumed that she would have said something. We'd spent enough time together that surely a boyfriend would have come up by now.

But then again, I'd never heard her talk about Olivia before, and the two of them were apparently best friends.

I stared down at the T-shirt in my hands. Maybe it was time to consider that I didn't know Collette nearly as well as I'd thought I did. But seriously, who was that blond guy sitting next to her?

How did she even meet him? He was wearing Oakwood colors so I went to school with him. Or did I? Man, my head was a mess.

"I've got to go find my parents," I said, not bothering to stick around while Ryan finished getting ready. I walked out into the hallway and scanned the crowd. No sign of a short brunette with curves to die for. The thought of her sitting up there in the stands, all cute and natural and genuine...

The smile on my lips died a quick death when I remembered the blond guy leaning over and her smiling at him and—

"Great game, son!" My dad's booming voice came from my left and I watched as the crowds parted for him like he was freakin' Mayor Moses. He was beaming at me with pride, my mother smiling more sedately as she followed along behind him with Chrissy.

My little sister slipped away from my mom the moment she saw me and I abandoned my Collette lookout as I swept her up in my arms for a bear hug when she crashed into me.

"You did great, Ethan!" She pressed her face into me and hugged me tight.

"Thanks, squirt." I messed up her hair. Right on cue, she glanced up at me, her nose wrinkled in annoyance.

I smelled my mother's expensive perfume before I felt her lips on my cheek. "You did great, sweetheart."

"Thanks, Mom."

And then my dad was next to me, giving me the sort of one-armed manly hug I never got except for times like this one—rare and fleeting moments when I'd actually managed to make him proud.

"That last touchdown," he was saying, "that was incredible." His face was alight with excitement like he was still reliving that moment.

My moment.

This wasn't the first time I wondered if my dad had any idea that the guy standing in front of him was his own man. That I was an individual in my own right and not some carbon copy he'd created so he could relive his glory days.

A group of cheerleaders jostled me on one side as more players came out of the locker room and into the already crowded hallway. It was getting hard to hear as people shouted over one another.

"Great job, Ethan." My friend Claire, one of the senior cheerleaders, gave me a quick hug as she squeezed past me.

"I need to talk to you, Son," my dad said to my left. His movement brought Claire closer to me and in the confusion, Claire pressed into me. I felt her giggle and I glanced down to give her a sympathetic smile and shrug. We'd been friends since Kindergarten. If not, this would have been embarrassing.

But just then one of the cheerleaders shifted and from the corner of my eye, I saw a flash of brown hair. Collette. I craned my neck to see if I'd been right, only to be met with Collette's furrowed brow. I didn't have to worry about her spotting me as well. Her eyes were fixed on me but she wasn't smiling. If anything, she looked hurt.

I raised a hand and beckoned her over. She jerked forward

quickly like she'd been shoved from behind, and that was when I saw Olivia behind her, pushing her toward me.

Well, at least one of them wanted to see me.

Fear had me scanning Collette's features, trying to figure out what she was thinking. The weird look. The wariness—it had to do with my last text. I knew it. I'd shown my hand when I'd asked her point blank if she had a boyfriend and now she was trying to figure out a nice way to tell me that she'd never seen me as anything more than a friend.

"Did you hear me, Son?" My father's voice lost its jovial tone. I whipped my head around to face him. Sure enough, he was all business once again. He placed a hand on my shoulder, his grip hard and unrelenting. "Good news, right?"

"Uh, what's the good news?"

I tried to sneak a glance over to my right but my dad was in my face. I could feel Collette though. After weeks of dancing together, our bodies were somehow in tune with each other. I tried to move toward her, acknowledge her so she wouldn't run off—

"Are you even listening?" my father snapped, all post-win good vibes officially gone.

"Oh, Jack, leave the boy alone," I heard my mom mutter. "You're making a scene."

His grip tensed one more time as I saw the internal struggle flash inside of him. But then, he sighed and dropped his hand from my shoulder. His *everything is perfect* smile returned. The threat of making a public spectacle got through to him because of course that was all that mattered here.

"What were you saying?" I asked.

I felt Collette brush against my side, hovering just behind me, waiting for me to acknowledge her.

"I *said...*" My dad drew the word out and it took everything in me not to shake him in frustration. *Just spit it out.* I had a girl to see. I needed to get a straight answer from her on whether or not she had a boyfriend, because if she did—well, I didn't know what I'd do, but the mere thought was killing me.

Not knowing was even worse.

"The recruiter from Yale was very impressed, I'll tell you that." My dad was once again happy, clearly pleased by whatever conversation he'd had with the scout. I'd zoned out for a second but caught up quickly. Recruit. Yale. All my dad's dreams were coming true. "He's coming to the fundraiser on Thursday night so you two will talk then."

I opened my mouth to give my perfunctory, "yes, sir" but stopped when his words registered. Thursday. That was the same night that Ryan's band was playing The Tailgate. "Um, actually Dad..."

He froze, his eyes fixed on mine. "What?"

The words got stuck in my throat. I could practically feel Collette tense beside me as she waited for me to continue. To say...something. Anything.

"Thursday night, I have plans."

He frowned in confusion. "Then change them."

"It's not that simple, I made a promise and—"

"I don't care what you promised." His voice was low. Little more than a snarl as he leaned in so his face was inches from mine. "This is important to me—you. How can you not see that? This is your future. It's all that matters."

"Jack," my mom hissed. I thought for a moment it was because she cared about sticking up for her only son but when I saw my mom's gaze flit around to the oblivious bystanders, I realized she didn't want a scene. Of course. Chrissy clutched my left hand and to my right I could feel Collette. I knew what she wanted me to say, but...

It wasn't that easy.

"I made a commitment," I repeated like it was somehow going to change my dad's mind.

"Then you will apologize and break it." The words came out harsh and over-pronounced. "I've given you too much leeway with your after school practices and all this ridiculous ballet crap. But this is non-negotiable. Do you hear me?"

He didn't move. Neither did I. Neither did Collette.

My jaw worked as I fought a wave of anger and humiliation that everyone around us was watching. That Collette was watching.

My dad wouldn't move away until I was defeated—I knew this. "Fine," I muttered.

My father's posture eased, and he straightened the collar of his jacket. "Good," he said, forcing a jovial tone once more. "Now, we'll let you get to your celebrations." He wrapped an arm around my mom's waist and placed a hand on Chrissy's shoulder. "You deserve it, Son."

They turned and walked away. Chrissy glanced behind her and gave me a soft smile. She was the only part of my family that I liked. And most times, her smile was what brought me back from the insanity that was my father.

But tonight, I knew I had to face someone else and no smile from Chrissy was going to change that.

I stared after my family, feeling the seconds tick by. I knew I needed to look down, to face Collette. I just wasn't ready. I knew she wasn't going to let this go. That wasn't the kind of relationship we had. But after our texts, I really wasn't sure what kind of relationship we had.

My life was a big, giant heap of crap.

When I did finally turn, I saw Olivia backing away with a wary look. Her gaze kept flicking from me down to Collette and then back up to me. I didn't have to see Collette to know she was upset. I could feel her anger. It was potent and pronounced.

"I'm just gonna...I'll be over..." And then Olivia was gone, darting down the hallway toward the exit as Collette and I turned to face each other.

Those big blue eyes were filled with so many emotions I couldn't begin to name them. I watched her swallow and then she looked away. "So...what? You're just going to bail on Ryan?"

I drew in an inhale with a hiss. This girl definitely didn't pull her punches. I scoffed as I shoved my hands into the front pockets of my jeans and shrugged. "I have to. I'm a Morrison." Saying Dad's line felt like acid on my tongue. It was lame and a cop-out but what else was I supposed to do? Her jaw worked as she crossed her arms over her chest. "You could have told him. You could have tried to explain."

I shook my head in frustration. Out of everyone I knew, I would have figured that Collette would understand why I had to bail. She understood the pressure I felt to please my father.

But what did I know? After all, I thought she was single and I was apparently very wrong about that. I was such a fool.

"Explain what? That I like playing guitar? What would that change? He still wouldn't have let me skip the most important meeting of my life."

Was I exaggerating? Maybe. But that was how my dad would see it. This was everything I'd been working toward. This was everything he'd been dreaming about.

"This is your first chance to play with the band. You've been practicing every day, to do what? Never play live?" she said, scowling up at me like I was the enemy here. "What's the point of practicing if no one will ever hear you play? Is that the kind of future you want?"

Was she serious? How could she say these things to me when she was doing the exact same?

It stung, hearing these words escape her lips. How could she ask me to pick between my future and music? How was this any different than what my father was doing?

"The meeting with the recruiter is my future," I shot back. I looked around, noticing the stares we were starting to get and let out a long exhale to relax. Why was I even defending myself? Of course I'd rather play with the band then stand around being scrutinized by my father's friends at his ridiculous party, but for some reason, her reaction to me had me on the defense.

This was stupid. We needed to talk, somewhere away from all the prying eyes.

"Come on," I said, snagging one of her hands and dragging her after me as I took off toward the locker rooms. There was a back exit that led directly to the parking lot but no one went out that way, preferring instead to gather up front to mingle and congratulate the team.

We turned two corners before she tugged her hand out of mine. "I don't need you to hold my hand." Her words sounded tough but her tone was soft. Broken.

I stopped to face her. "What is going on here?"

Her face was flushed, dark curls escaping from her ponytail and framing her face. She looked so pretty...or she would have if she wasn't shooting death glares in my direction. "You're dragging me down a dark hallway."

I huffed. "Don't play dumb. You're pissed at me—"

"Of course I am," she interrupted. "You had the perfect opportunity to step up to your dad and tell the truth for once in your life and—"

"For once in my life?" I echoed. "Since when am I the bad

guy here? Yeah, I've been lying to my dad about our private sessions, but you've been lying too."

Her mouth snapped shut and I felt an inexplicable surge of guilt. "It's not the same," she said.

"How?" I threw my hand out to the side. "Seriously, how is this not the same?"

Her cheeks turned red with anger as she took a step forward and jabbed me in the chest. "It's totally different for you. You could pursue your dreams if you wanted to." She shook her head. "Your dad's opinion is the only thing standing in your way. If you wanted to be a musician, you could go to Juilliard."

I stood there stunned by the sheer anger in her voice. At first, I thought her anger was because of me, but now, I was beginning to think this was about something completely different. Something I didn't quite understand, but I wanted to. Oh, how I wanted to understand this beautiful, complex woman in front of me. I took in a breath, trying to calm my anger before I spoke.

"You're right it is different for me, because I don't have dreams of making this my future or my career. You do," I said. "Yale is my future. Juilliard is yours."

"Don't you get it?" Her expression was pinched with anger, and the pain in her eyes was hard to witness. "I can't be a dancer." She gestured to her body. "I will never be a dancer—"

"You don't know that." Why did she keep saying this about herself? She was amazing, she had to know that.

"I do," she whispered. Her anger had morphed into pain. Deep, soul-crushing pain. It was etched on her face. "I've been told that on a daily basis for years by people who know."

"Well, they're wrong. They're idiots, and—"

Her snort of disgust cut me off. "You don't know anything about my world so please don't lecture me."

"I wasn't trying to—"

"You live in this perfect world where everyone falls all over you." She wrapped her arms around her middle. "Including me."

I almost missed the last part because she'd said it so quietly. Almost to herself. My heartbeat changed from one of frustration to one of hope. But doubt crept in just as quickly and I began to fear I was making things up in my head.

But I needed to know. "What did you say?" I asked.

She stared down at the ground and frustration had me clenching my hands into fists to keep from shaking her. "Why didn't you reply to my last text?"

Her head shot up. "What?"

I thrust a hand through my hair, which was still wet from the showers. I took a deep breath and tried for calm. "Did you read it?"

She shook her head, her eyes focused on my T-shirt now, like she couldn't quite meet my eyes.

"I asked if you have a boyfriend."

Her eyes flickered up. "Were you mocking me?"

I narrowed my eyes as I tried to make sense of this non sequitur. "What? When?"

She licked her lips and glanced away. "Forget it. I shouldn't even care."

"Care about what? What am I missing here?"

"You know, I thought..." I watched her swallow and try again. "We've been hanging out alone so much that I guess I just forgot..."

I stepped closer, gripping her arms so she would look up at me. "What are you trying to say?"

"I saw you with those cheerleaders," she said. "That's the kind of girl you like, right? I don't know why I thought..." She closed her eyes and took a step back so my hands fell to my sides.

I had this horrible feeling like I was watching her slip away even though she was standing right here. "Collette Boucher, do you or do you not have a boyfriend?"

She bit her lip and then she looked up at me and my heart freakin' took a tumble off a cliff. I was falling. My whole body felt like it was free-falling.

"No," she said softly, and relief nearly knocked me over. "But—"

I gripped her arms again and I pulled her close. I didn't wait to hear her buts. I wanted to feel her lips on mine. I wanted...her.

I let instinct take over as I stepped forward and cradled her cheek with my hand. I leaned forward, desperate to show her in one kiss everything that I felt.

Collette was quick-witted and snarky, but this was one conversation I knew I could win.

I pressed my lips to hers and electricity shot throughout my entire body. From the gasp that escaped her lips, I knew she felt it too. At first, she was hesitant, like she didn't know what to do, but then, her hands made their way to my shoulders and then the back of my neck.

I took that as my cue to deepen the kiss. Everything about Collette, from the way she tasted to the way her body fit perfectly against mine, made me realize that out of the mess that was my life, Collette was the only perfect thing that existed.

I kissed her deeper, slanting my lips over hers as a surge of something so pure hit me, it had my head spinning. My arms ached with the realization that at some point, I was going to have to let her go. I slid my hands to her back and held her tight, reveling in the feel of her soft skin and her warm lips and the sweet sincerity in the way she kissed me back.

I could have kissed her like that forever, but she pulled back. She blinked once. Twice. And then she was staring up at me with wide eyes that were filled with...

Fear.

My chest tightened as I worried what that meant. I could feel her pulling away and there was nothing I could do about it. I went to reach for her but she took another step back, shaking her head. "I don't...I don't know what that was."

"You're amazing, Collette." I took a step forward but she started backpedaling quickly.

"No, I'm not," she said. "Please stop." Her hands were raised as if she were worried I'd keep advancing.

"You are." A strange sort of desperation crept into my voice as I tried to make her see how I've been feeling these past few weeks. Surely she'd felt it too, right?

She had to have felt it too.

Her eyes met mine and she shook her head. "I'm not amazing. You don't know what you're saying. I'm not..." Her voice trailed off as tears brimmed her eyelids. Then she shook her head and glanced up at me. I could see the determination in her gaze. "You barely even know me and I...I definitely don't know you."

She took off before I could stop her but her words stayed. They lingered and they stung.

Hurt lanced through me at what I knew she'd meant. I'd let her down when I hadn't stood up to my dad. I'd failed her and now she saw who I really was.

She'd seen the real me...and she wanted nothing to do with him.

TWELVE

COLLETTE

Thankfully, Olivia didn't pepper me with questions when I met her at my car after I ran full speed away from Ethan. She remained quiet as I drove her home even though I had tears running down my cheeks.

As I idled next to the dormitory, she turned and gave me a hug.

"Love you, Collette," she said as she pulled back and shot me a quick smile.

I nodded and blew out my breath. "I'll tell you tomorrow," I said as I stifled a sob.

Olivia nodded. "I know you will. When you're ready, I'm here."

I shot her a thankful smile and she saluted me as she grabbed the door handle and stepped out. I waited for her to walk into the dorm before I pulled away from the curb and merged into traffic.

Mom was asleep when I got home. I tiptoed through the kitchen. I didn't want to wake her up. Mom and I didn't have the strongest relationship, but I feared if she saw me crying, she'd ask why.

And I didn't want to tell her.

She knew nothing of Ethan and I wanted to keep it that way.

I grabbed a water bottle from the fridge as I passed by. Crying made me thirsty and I was pretty sure I wasn't finished for the night. Just as I stepped back to shut the fridge door, something caught my eye.

An invitation. To Ethan's dad's fundraiser.

I glowered at it. Mr. Morrison definitely left an impression on you. There was no way I was going to that. Not after the way he treated Ethan. Even though I was a mess when it came to my relationship with Ethan, I did have loyalties and out of spite, I wasn't going to give Mr. Morrison the time of day.

My heart ached so I pushed the idea of the party from my mind. It only led to frustration as I thought of Ethan's decision that his father's bidding was more important than following his dream.

Once I got into my room, I shut the door quietly and flopped onto my bed. I let my sobs and tears soak into my comforter as I thought back to Ethan and our fight. The things he said, the things I said. They were real and painful. I didn't mean to make him feel bad, but he had to know the truth. He was more than what his dad thought he was.

And then there was that kiss. I'd been blown away by the electricity that raced between us. It was like touching a live wire. Scary yet mesmerizing.

I reached up and touched my lips. I could still feel his lips pressed against mine. I could still feel the way he'd pressed against every part of my body—my body that I'd hated for so long. He'd touched me like he didn't care. He'd touched me like he wanted to *feel* me.

And that scared me. More than anything I'd ever felt before.

How could he love me when I couldn't even love myself?

I sighed as I flipped to my back and draped my arm over my eyes.

"He can't," I whispered into the darkness.

Ethan didn't know what he was doing when he kissed me. When he told me I was amazing. He didn't know what was hiding underneath all of my layers. He'd been blinded by his excitement to play guitar at the studio that he didn't see what was so plainly displayed in front of him.

I wasn't the cheerleader I'd seen hugging him. I wasn't Bianca. I wasn't even a ballerina.

I was a wannabe who would never be able to perform. I was a fool who thought that dancing in the shadows meant I was born to be a dancer.

Obviously, I wasn't born to be anything, let alone a ballerina. Fate kept telling me that over and over again, yet I was too dense to listen.

My phone chimed. I pulled my arm down and stared up at the ceiling. It was probably Olivia, checking in on me. She was worried, no doubt. I would be too if I were her. I'd never been much of a crier but tonight I'd more than made up for it. If I didn't answer, she'd probably break the dorm curfew to come over here. Which meant, she'd get in trouble and I'd have to explain to my mom why my eyes were bloodshot and my comforter was soggy.

I reached down and pulled my phone from my hoodie pocket. I clicked it on and my heart stopped beating.

It was a text from Ethan.

I swallowed a few times, trying to calm my nerves. All I could read was the first line of the text that read, "I'm sorry."

After that, I'd need to access the text to read the rest.

Did I want to read it?

What if he was texting to say, "I'm sorry. I should have never kissed you" or worse...what if he was texting to say goodbye?

Was that something I wanted to read?

I took in a shuddering breath as I tried to calm my mind. If that was what he'd written, I'd be fine with it. After all, our relationship was doomed to end at some point. Who cared if it happened right now?

If anything, he was doing me a favor.

So I put on my big girl panties and typed in my password and clicked on the text.

Ethan: I'm sorry. I should have never kissed you when you weren't ready. I was confused and angry. Can you forgive me?

I stared at his words. My eyes had seen them, but my brain couldn't process what he'd said. Nowhere in the text was the word *mistake,* I should have never even met you, I was an idiot, or ewwwww (yes, with that many w's.)

He was just sorry that he pushed me. That was all.

Tears clung to my eyelids as I stared at the screen. Ethan was an incredible guy. Too bad I didn't deserve him. If I were going to cast anyone as the Ron to my Hermione, it would be Ethan.

Ethan: I know I let you down. Back there with my dad. I'm sorry about that too.

Guilt swept over me so quickly it hurt. I gripped the phone harder, my heart aching over everything I'd said to him—the judgy tone, the harsh accusations—and everything he *hadn't* said.

He could have called me a hypocrite. He could have pointed out that I was the coward who was hiding away in a studio after dark because I couldn't face my mother.

But he didn't say any of that because he was too nice for his own good.

Yale is my future, Juilliard is yours.

He still didn't get it. The guy still believed that I could overcome all the odds and become a successful ballerina. Right now I didn't know if that belief in me was insanely sweet or ridiculously naive, but I did know that I shouldn't have punished him for it.

My phone chimed again before I could respond.

Ethan: You're probably asleep, so I'll stop harassing you. I'm just worried I ruined everything. Please text me back when you get this.

And then a few seconds later another text came in.

Ethan: I can't lose you as a friend.

Friend. I swallowed as my emotions threatened to suffocate me. He wanted me as his friend. I'd known as much, but seeing it spelled out was the reality check I'd needed.

He wanted to forget that kiss and go back to being friends, that much was clear. Not a surprise, really. But what did I want? I didn't want to be his friend—or at least, not just his friend. It was time I just admitted that to myself.

But the thought that it could be more? That he could honestly want more? That was too hard to swallow. It was a daydream, just like Juilliard. The truth was, he could have any girl he wanted. He'd kissed me, yes, but he'd said himself that he'd been confused.

I stared at the phone, trying to figure out what I should say, but in the end, it was a no-brainer. *I can't lose you as a friend.* His words made me want to cry all over again. I may have wanted more, but I also loved what we had. I didn't want to lose him as a friend, either. He mattered way too much to me even if *Ethette* (I may have come up with a celebrity name for us) wasn't meant to be.

I took a deep breath and started to type.

Me: I forgive you. Truce?

I held my breath as the three dots began to dance.

Ethan: Truce. Meet you at the studio on Monday?

I sent him a GIF of a man saluting.

He sent back a laughing emoji.

I curled onto my side as I set my phone down next to me. Sure, I had major hangups and sure, I was an emotional basket case. But I still had my friend and that was all that mattered.

My phone chimed and I picked it back up.

Ethan: Can I ask you something?

Me: Sure

I waited, feeling a little nervous about what he was going to ask me.

Ethan: Don't take this the wrong way, but was that your first kiss?

I almost choked on my tongue as I moved to sit up. How was I supposed to respond to that? I didn't want to seem like a loser, but then again, if he was asking, then he knew the answer. Which meant it had been bad.

Realizing that if I lied, it meant more than I wanted it to, I decided to be honest.

Me: Yes

I held my breath as I waited for him to respond.

Ethan: Huh.

What did that mean? I closed my eyes as I rubbed my temples. This wasn't good. Oh, this wasn't good.

Me: Was it that obvious?

Ethan: What? No. Just…nothing. Forget I asked.

Oh no, now it was on. He couldn't just ask me something like that and then end the conversation. If he was my friend and we were going to try to make this work as friends, he needed to be honest with me.

Me: This is not fair. You can't just leave me hanging like that.

The dancing dots mocked me as they appeared and then disappeared more times than I could count. It left me to imagine what he could possibly be struggling to say. Whatever it was, it couldn't be good.

Me: Ethan, you're scaring me

Thankfully, his next response came faster than his previous ones.

Ethan: Oh, sorry. It wasn't bad.

Now I was completely confused. Was he saying my kiss wasn't bad? What did that mean?

Me: You know how to give a girl a complex.

Ethan: I don't want to do that, so let me start over. Your kiss was good. I was just surprised when you said it was your first.

My cheeks warmed as I read his last sentence. I blinked a few times as I tried to process what he said. Sure, our kiss had been a mistake, but it wasn't because I was a bad kisser.

And even though I didn't want to admit it, the fact that he'd enjoyed our kiss made my entire body tingle and I couldn't fight the smile that played on my lips. A sense of satisfaction flooded my body as I rolled to my back and stared up at my screen.

If I was going to have my first kiss with anyone, I was glad that it was Ethan. He was my friend and he knew me more than anyone else—well, besides Olivia. The fact that he wanted to kiss me and then complimented me on it meant a lot.

Me: Thanks

Ethan: And me? Do you want to say something to me?

I chewed my bottom lip as I thought back to our kiss. It was hot. Mind blowing. I was pretty sure he'd changed me more than I cared to admit. I doubt there was another guy on this planet that could make me feel what Ethan had.

But I couldn't say any of that. Not when we were supposed to be just friends.

So I settled with something less exposing.

Me: Eh

Ethan: ???

I sent a shrugging emoji.

Ethan: Talk about giving someone a complex. This wasn't my first time. You have me doubting my ability. Doubting if the Earth is round.

I giggled as I read it. Well, I didn't want to do that. Before I could respond, his next text came in.

Ethan: Don't answer that. I'm not sure I want to know one way or the other. Just know, I get a lot better.

Heat raced through my body and yet I shivered. I didn't doubt that kissing Ethan got better than what it had been. There were a lot of things I had felt in that one kiss and if this was just the beginning...I sighed.

I didn't want to admit it but I wanted to know more. And I wanted the guy who taught me everything to be Ethan.

Too bad it would never happen again.

Me: I'll keep that in mind for all of your future girlfriends.

I hoped that was all I needed to say to squelch his assumption that there would be a next time.

Ethan: Good night, friend Collette

I smiled. I felt victorious in our conversation.

Me: Good night, friend Ethan.

I waited for a minute or two to see if Ethan would text me back, but he never did so I rolled off my bed and plugged in my phone. After I brushed my teeth and washed my face, I returned to my room feeling a million times better.

I walked over to my phone, regret settled in my stomach. I hated how I'd left things with Olivia. So I turned on my phone.

Me: Sorry I was a dud tonight. I'll tell you tomorrow, 'kay? Movies?

Olivia: You don't need to apologize and yes, the movies. Noon?

I sent her a thumbs up and then left my phone to crawl onto my bed and curl up under my covers. I sighed as I closed my eyes.

Now, if I could only convince my heart and head that Ethan and I were only friends, then I'd be golden. But I doubted that was possible. Especially since right now, all I could think about was Ethan's hands on my body and his lips pressed against mine.

I had a feeling once I entered dream land, he was going to be the main star of my dreams and when I was unconscious, I wasn't able to tell myself to get a grip.

And even though I knew it should be a problem, if I were really honest, it wasn't.

Because in my dreams, I could have what I really wanted. Ethan.

I WOKE up in the middle of the night, dying of thirst. My throat felt like sandpaper as I flung the covers from my body and slipped my feet to the cold floor. I winced as my feet took a few seconds to adjust.

I wrapped my blanket around my shoulders and stood. I tiptoed out of my room, making a point to avoid the creaky floorboards. I winced as I stepped on one. My entire body tensed as I waited for Mom's door to open.

It never did.

After a few seconds, I blew out my breath, tucked my hair behind my ear, and made a beeline toward the kitchen. As soon as I was in front of the fridge, I pulled open the door and grabbed a water bottle.

"Couldn't sleep either?"

Mom's voice made me scream and drop to the floor. Once reality set it that we weren't getting robbed, embarrassment coursed through me. I scrambled to stand and shut the fridge door.

"You scared me," I mumbled as I turned to face her. She was sitting at the table with stacks of papers around her and a coffee mug in the middle of it all. Her hair was pulled up into a messy bun and her glasses were perched on the tip of her nose.

She looked tired...and stressed.

Not wanting our status quo to be our future relationship, I fought the urge to run back to my room and walked over to the table and sat down. I cracked the lid on my water bottle and took a sip.

Mom was watching me with raised eyebrows and parted lips. Like she wasn't sure what to make of what I was doing.

"Light reading?" I asked as I scanned the top paper. There were a lot of numbers all over it.

Mom sighed as she leaned her elbows on the tabletop and rubbed her temples. "I couldn't sleep."

I nodded. "Me neither." I took another sip of water as I studied Mom. She had dark circles under her eyes and the spark I used to see when she danced—or even talked about dancing—was gone. "You okay? You know, you can talk to me."

I winced. Since when did I sound like a school guidance

counselor? This was why I stayed away from emotional conversations. I stunk at them.

Mom leaned back and tapped her fingers on the table. Then she leaned in and sighed as she took a sip of her coffee. "How well do you know Ethan Morrison?"

I furrowed my brow. Why was she asking me that? Did she know something? "He dances with Bianca. I know that." I tried to calm my pounding heart, hoping she wouldn't pick up on the fact that he and I kissed hours ago.

And that I may have feelings for him.

I cleared my throat, hoping my mom wouldn't pick up on my failed attempt at indifference. "Why?"

She studied me and then shook her head. "Never mind. He just called me earlier and asked me something..." Her voice trailed off. I raised my eyebrows at her ominous statement.

"What did he ask?" I hated how desperate I sounded. But I needed to know what they'd talked about. Was it me?

Mom blinked a few times as she turned to study me. Then she shook her head. "Nothing. It was...never mind." She sighed as she pinched the bridge of her nose. Her shoulders slumped.

I decided to let it go. I doubted it was about me. Guys didn't normally call up random girl's parents for just a chat. It most likely had to do with the fact that the team was tired of taking lessons. They wanted to get out of them and sent Ethan in as tribute.

"Can I help? I mean, with whatever is stressing you out. I'd like to help."

Mom tipped her head to study me and then sighed. "It's just, things are bad. Funding is drying up and I don't know where I'm going to get more." She cleared her throat and I could see tears brimming her lids. "If this thing with Juilliard is a bust, I think I'll have to shut the doors."

I stared at her with my lips parted. I wanted to protest. I

wanted to tell her not to worry. But what did I know? I didn't know the first thing about running a ballet academy.

"Mom, seriously?" I leaned in, hoping I'd misheard her.

"I thought maybe opening our school to outside classes might help. Specialized classes like what we're doing for the Oakwood football team, but...I don't think anyone is happy with the way that's going." Mom pinched her lips together. "I just don't know what else to do. Juilliard calling me was the sort of Hail Mary I was hoping for. But if they don't pick someone from our school, it's the end." She tipped her head up and closed her eyes as she blew her breath out. "We'll be done. Finished. Closed."

My chest felt as if there was a vise squeezing it to the point of bursting. Sure, I didn't take dance classes, but that didn't mean that I wanted the place to close. The school was my home and so many girls depended on it staying open.

I reached out and rested my hand on her clasped ones. She glanced up at me with a pseudo smile. She was hurting. I could see it. Feel it.

"It will work out, Mom," I said as I held her gaze.

She freed one of her hands so she could pat my hand. "Thanks, Collette. You always know how to make me feel better."

I smiled, hoping she'd feel my confidence. That I could somehow make up for her lack of confidence. She was an amazing teacher and an incredible dancer. Anyone who worked with her would succeed. That was a fact.

"You know what you're doing, Mom. You can do this."

A tear slipped down her cheek. "Thanks, Collette." She smiled, this time a genuine one. "I'm not sure what I'd do without you. Since your father left, I've always worried I was failing you." She reached out and rested her hand on my cheek. "But you're a fighter and I love that about you."

"Thanks, Mom," I said. My voice had turned husky as emotions choked my throat. If she only knew what I had been planning, she wouldn't say what she just did.

If she only knew that I had been contemplating signing up for the Juilliard audition against her wishes, she'd take her words back.

I wasn't a great daughter. I was selfish. Mom didn't set the standards for a ballerina and she just wanted me to be realistic. My auditioning wouldn't change anything, and my almost-certain failure wasn't going to help anyone.

And yet, here I sat, thinking I knew better. And I didn't.

If I loved my mom then I wouldn't ask her to sacrifice her dream of running the academy just to play to my delusion that I *might* be able to get into Juilliard. If I loved my mom, I would step back. I would let the Juilliard recruits only see our best chance—someone like Bianca or Eve. To win a coveted spot on the Juilliard stage and finally put Academie de Ballet back on the map where it belonged.

If I cared about my mom, I would be a better daughter because in the end, the only thing that matters is the relationships you have. And if I lost my mother, I'd have nothing.

And that was the last thing I wanted.

Dancing wouldn't make me happy if it made my mom miserable, and from the way she was hunched over the table with stress etched on her face, she would be heartbroken to lose the studio.

As someone with a perpetually broken heart, I wouldn't wish that on anyone. If giving up dance made my mom truly happy, then I'd do it. I would walk away.

I'd put on a smile and cheer on the other dancers as they tried out. I'd be supportive as they got opportunities I only dreamed of.

In the end, dancing was just that. A dream I could never make a reality.

It was time I started accepting that. Before a lot of the people I cared about got hurt.

Before I started down a path I couldn't come back from.

I was at a crossroads and I needed to make the right decision. Even if it broke my entire soul to accept my fate, I was going to accept that Juilliard and I would never be.

I loved my mom too much to perpetuate this fantasy.

THIRTEEN

ETHAN

I hated that I was nervous as I drove to the academy after school on Monday. It was the first time I was going to see Collette after our kiss and I was supposed to play it cool.

And I was. I was the cool guy.

But not anymore. Things with Collette had changed and I was fairly certain that it wasn't going to go back. No matter how much I tried to convince myself that things could be the same, it wasn't possible.

We were definitely more than friends. But I couldn't think like that. If I did, I'd lose her. I was still uncertain as to why. Collette was a puzzle I was determined to figure out if it killed me.

When you had something as great as Collette, you worked hard for it. And like my dad always said, Morrisons weren't quitters. And I wasn't going to start now.

Even so, I was starting to second guess what I'd set in motion. I mean, there were grand gestures and then there were epic fails, and I was starting to worry that the surprise I'd planned for today would be the latter.

I gripped the steering wheel long after I parked, giving myself the sort of inner pep talk I gave myself before a game.

After I exited my car and crossed the street, I took the front steps two at a time. I straightened my duffle bag on my shoulder as I moved to pull open the front door.

"Oh good. You're here."

Olivia's voice startled me. I yelped and turned to see her familiar dark eyes and curly black hair. She had a sucker in her mouth and her eyebrows were raised as she ran her gaze over me.

I liked Olivia but she scared me.

"Hey," I said. "How's it going?"

She waved away my lame attempt at small-talk and grabbed my arm as she pulled me to the side. "We need to talk."

I moved to follow her. As soon as we were around the building, she turned and poked my shoulder. "Why did you kiss Collette?" she asked and then folded her arms. She looked like a teacher punishing a student.

Not sure what I was supposed to say, I shoved my hands into the front pockets of my jeans and shrugged. "It felt like the right thing to do at the time." That made me sound like a prick and from her raised eyebrows, Olivia agreed.

I sighed and raised my hand to run it through my hair and down to my neck. "Why do you think?" I held her gaze so she could feel how serious I was about Collette.

Olivia narrowed her eyes. "Hmm, that's what I thought."

I felt exposed and raw that Olivia now knew this about me. About us. "Did Collette tell you?" Did I dare hope that Collette might have talked about this with Olivia? That maybe it meant more to her than she was letting on.

Olivia snorted. "We're best friends, so, yeah. She told me."

I swallowed as I tried to push down the fear that had crept

up inside of me. I didn't know how to read Olivia and I hated this feeling of limbo.

She must have seen my fear because a moment later, she sighed and waved her hand at me. "Don't worry, she likes you too." Olivia tapped her chin like she was thinking.

I couldn't fight the smile that emerged on my lips. My heart was pounding in my chest and I felt like I was about to float away. Collette *did* like me. I knew it. And she liked me enough to tell her friend.

See? This would all work out. I'd show her how I felt, I'd prove to her that I was there for her, and then I'd kiss her until she forgot all about whatever hangups she was holding onto to push me away.

"She said that?" I asked, hoping that I didn't sound too eager. "She told you she liked me?"

Olivia blinked a few times as if she were returning to the present. She shook her head. "Collette didn't need to say anything. I know my friend. She likes you."

Well, that took some of the wind out of my sails. I'd rather hear that Collette couldn't stop talking about me. But it appeared that she was just as tight-lipped with Olivia as she was with me.

Maybe I was moving too quickly...again. Maybe she needed more time. Maybe I shouldn't try to push her into something she's not ready for...

I needed to see Collette and I needed to see her now. If I didn't, these doubts would be the death of me.

I had a plan, now I had to see it through.

It was too late for second guessing. I'd taken two steps toward the studio when Olivia stopped me.

"Why are you walking away from me?" she asked. With a smirk, she added, "Do I make you nervous?"

I nodded. "A little bit, yeah."

She smiled. "Good. Then you know I could destroy you if you hurt my friend."

"I'm not going to hurt Collette," I said. She had to know that.

She narrowed her eyes and then nodded. "I believe you. Or, at least..." She stopped as though she were considering her next words carefully. "I don't think you'd *intentionally* hurt her."

Her words made me wince. I didn't want to hurt Collette... period. Intentionally or otherwise.

"Look," Olivia said as she crossed her arms. "I know Collette seems strong and she acts like nothing bothers her, but she's not...unbreakable."

I nodded, my heart in my throat as I thought of the look in her eyes before she'd run away. It had taken me a little while to figure it out, but the more I'd replayed that entire incident, the more I'd seen the truth behind her actions.

It wasn't me she'd been scared of, it was herself.

It was the same look she got when she talked about her dreams of dancing—this sort of bittersweet longing. It was the look of wanting something you know you can't have.

I had to believe she felt this connection between us. I had to trust that she wanted it too.

Otherwise...

I swallowed down a tidal wave of fear. Well, otherwise I was about to have my heart handed to me on a plate.

Olivia shifted, her eyes darting away guiltily. "She has these insecurities..." she started. "Between her mother and being raised in this world..." She shook her head as she trailed off, clearly at a loss for words.

"I know," I said.

Olivia's gaze darted back to mine, her eyes widening in surprise.

"I get it," I said.

She studied me for a while, like she could read something in my eyes. Whatever she saw there, she seemed to come to some sort of conclusion. With a short nod, she said, "Yeah, I guess maybe you do."

The thing was I did get it. I mean, I didn't fully understand Collette's body issues, because those just seemed crazy to me, but I understood living in a parent's shadow. I got how hard it was to figure out who you really were when you spent most of your life living up to expectations—or living down to expectations, as the case may be.

I understood how hard it was to find yourself when everyone around you looked at you like they already knew exactly who you were.

I also knew that Collette had helped me figure out who I was—or at least, who I wanted to be. And I wanted to be the guy who did the same for her.

But first, I had to find her. I had to talk to her...and I had to say a prayer that she didn't punch me in the face when I told her what I'd done.

I started to turn away when Olivia rested a hand on my arm. "Don't tell her I said anything. She'd kill me."

I nodded and raised my right hand in the Boy Scout salute. "I promise."

Olivia hesitated and then dropped her hand. I made my way to the front door and pulled it open and disappeared inside. My heart was pounding as I scoured the studios in search of Collette.

Collette was the sexiest, most beautiful girl I knew. She took my breath away and I hated that she doubted that in herself. She needed to see herself in a new light—she needed to see herself like I saw her.

Just as I passed by the far end studio window, I stopped.

Collette was standing in the center of the room. She had on her leotard and tights and was practicing a move. I loved how her nose crinkled as she flung her foot out and turned. She spun around and stopped.

I thought she looked amazing, but she must have not done something right because a moment later, she blew the loose strands of hair that had fallen out of her bun from her face and tried it again.

Just as she moved to twirl, her gaze fell on me. Her lips tipped up into a shy smile as I raised my hand to wave.

She motioned for me to come into the room and I did. I pulled open the door just as she rushed over to the chair next to the wall and grabbed her sweatshirt. I used to think it was cute that she liked to wear them, but now? They were just a sign of her insecurities.

But she slipped it on before I could stop her. She walked over to me with her wide blue eyes that danced with excitement, and my heart ached for the sadness I knew she held within herself.

I wanted to prove to her right here, right now, that she was incredible.

"Where's your guitar?" she asked as she glanced around.

I shrugged as I slipped off my duffle bag and took a step toward her. "It's in my car. I can get it later."

She furrowed her brow. "Later? No, you practice first, remember?" She took a step back as I advanced on her.

I held her gaze, hoping she would feel everything that I was trying to say. Everything I felt. I doubted that she just wanted to be friends. I was almost positive that she was scared. And I could work with scared.

"Not today," I said as I reached out and grasped the edge of her hoodie that she had wrapped around her body like a robe. I was tired of her hatred of her body and I was going to show her what I saw. What I *only* saw.

"Ethan, what are you doing?" she asked as her gaze filled with fear.

"Why do you always wear this when we practice?" I asked, allowing my voice to deepen as I grasped the other side of her hoodie.

Collette's cheeks heated as she kept her arms wrapped around her stomach. "I get cold," she said as she stepped back.

I shook my head. "I don't believe that." I moved closer just to see her eyes widen.

"I like the way it feels on my skin."

I shook my head. "Try again."

Tears brimmed her eyelids and I wanted to fix what she felt was so broken inside of her. What I saw was perfection and it killed me that she didn't see the same.

"What do you want me to say?" she asked as she studied me.

I met her gaze and took in the pain that she held there. I could see the turmoil that was tearing her apart. And then, I realized that the only way to reach Collette—to really speak to her—was to dance.

"That you'll dance with me? Without"—I waved to her hoodie—"this."

She glanced down and stared at her hoodie. Then she glanced up at me. A tear slipped down her cheek as she studied me. "Ethan, I can't."

I reached up and wiped it away. Then I smiled at her, hoping I came across as encouraging instead of creepy.

"You can," I said. Then I turned and made my way over to the stereo. I plugged in my phone and found *Fix You* by Coldplay.

The beginning chords began to play and I let the notes flow

through me. I hesitated and then turned to see Collette standing in the middle of the dance floor. She had her arms still tucked around her body and her head tipped down.

For a moment, I wondered if I'd pushed her too far. That I was going to lose her if I didn't backpedal right now.

But then, slowly, she began to open her arms. She pulled at the sides of the hoodie and allowed it to slip to the floor. Her eyes remained closed and I could see her entire body tense as she stood there.

Not wanting her to feel vulnerable and scared, I made my way over to her. When I neared, I reached out and ran my hand down her arm, just so she knew I was there. I felt her tighten and goosebumps appeared on her skin.

But she didn't move. She didn't leave.

I situated myself behind her and hesitated, listening to the beat of the music like Collette taught me. Then, forcing confidence to the surface, I raised her hand and brought it to my neck. Collette moved with the motion of her arm, tipping her face in my direction.

Then slowly and tenderly, I began to run my fingers down the inner part of her arm then to her ribs. Warmth exploded through my body as I rested my hand just above her waist, waiting for her to grab it.

I felt her tense as my fingers lingered and for a moment, I feared I'd gone too far. But then her fingers found mine and I pulled her so that she spun out and then back in. Her hands sprawled out across my chest and I wondered if she could feel my pounding heart.

Our breathing was heavy as she held her stance. She was raised up on her toes as she waited for my move. I glanced down to see her looking at me. I could feel the fear flickering in her eyes.

But I wasn't going to back down. I wanted Collette. In more ways than one. And I was going to show her.

So I slid my hand from her back, to her waist and I lingered there. Then I bounced down on my knees and she took that as my signal. She held onto my shoulders as I lifted her up. Her legs were taut as I swept her from one side of my body to the other side.

Then I braced myself as I dipped down and Collette flung her legs up. That brought our faces inches from each other. I held her gaze. I held this position. I wanted her to see that she was beautiful. That to me, she was everything.

And to my surprise, she didn't break the connection that was zipping between the two of us. Her eyes were wide and I could tell she was searching for my disgust or fear, but she was never going to find it. Instead, I hoped all she saw was admiration for everything about her.

I slowly lowered her to the ground and we fell into a rhythm. With every beat, every movement, I could feel her loosen. That the wall that she'd built up around her was crumbling and it gave me the confidence to truly touch her.

When I dragged my hand around her middle as she spun around me, she didn't shy away. Or when I followed behind her, helping to reach greater heights with each leap, she stayed strong. I could feel her confidence build.

And when I waited at the other end of the studio for her to run and leap, I could see her genuine smile as she met my gaze. This was the Collette I'd fallen in love with. She was magnificent.

"Ready?" she mouthed in a teasing way.

I flexed my muscles in an exaggerated manner and then winked as I nodded and I bent down, holding my arms out. I would always be ready to catch her.

She nodded and then slowly began to spin. Her leg flung

out and then back in like a spinning top my grandpa had given me when I was a kid.

Then, just as I lost myself in her movements, she stopped and rushed across the studio and straight into my arms.

I didn't hesitate as I wrapped my hands around her middle and lifted her into the air. Her arms were spread out and from where I was standing, I could see the sheer joy on her face.

The song ended and I slowly lowered her to the ground. I held her close as I stared down at her. My hands lingered on her waist and she didn't move to break the contact.

Instead, she rested her hands on my chest. She was staring at them, our breaths matching cadence.

"Ethan," she whispered.

"Yeah?"

She tipped her head back so she could meet my gaze. She chewed her lip as she stared at me. Then her gaze slipped down to my lips and I knew what she wanted. It was exactly what I hadn't been able to get out of my mind since Friday night.

Kissing Collette had meant more to me than I'd allowed myself to admit. And now that I knew she wanted it too, I wasn't going to hold back.

I dipped down to brush my lips against hers. But before they met, a voice snapped us apart.

"What is going on here?"

Collette sprang away from me like I'd electrocuted her. We both spun around to face the doorway where Bianca was scowling at us in confusion. "Seriously," she said with a shake of her head. "What on earth is going on here?"

"Uh..." Collette looked like she was scrambling to form words, her eyes still wide with shock.

"We're rehearsing," I said. I hoped my tone conveyed 'end of story, now leave us alone.' If it did, Bianca didn't get the hint.

"Rehearsing?" Her brow was furrowed in confusion as she looked from me to Collette and then back again. Her eyes took me in from head to toe and her confusion morphed into amusement.

"Wait a second, don't tell me you're going to audition for Juilliard's *dance department?*"

She was talking to me, but Collette misunderstood and started to answer. "No, of course not," she said.

But Bianca ignored her, all of her focus on me. "Ms. Boucher said you wanted an audition slot for music, not dance."

Oh no.

I felt Collette's stare on the side of my face as Bianca's words registered.

Oh crap.

Collette turned to face me. I could see her reflection in the mirror but I couldn't quite bring myself to look at her. "What is she talking about?" Collette's voice was barely a whisper. I hated how she sounded so betrayed.

Crap, crap, crap! This was so not how she was supposed to find out. I had a plan. It involved a speech—a good one. One that explained in detail how I'd gotten her an audition slot and would be by her side the whole time.

I would tell her how talented she was, and how I believed in her, and—

"He didn't tell you?" Bianca asked Collette. "Ethan here begged your mom for a slot, and of course she said yes to the mayor's son."

She rolled her eyes as she said it, but I was too busy trying to think of a way to explain.

"Ethan?" Collette said. "What is she talking about?"

I turned to face her. "I can explain."

Her cheeks were turning pink, a sure sign she was getting angry. "Explain what, exactly?"

"Uh..." I darted a look over to Bianca. A silent appeal for some privacy.

She leaned against the door frame with a little smile like this was the best entertainment she'd seen all day. "So wait, Collette doesn't know that you're asking for favors from her mom? That you're touting your leverage as the mayor's son to get ahead?"

I looked back to Collette, hating the fact that her happiness was gone now, replaced by suspicion and anger and...fear. That fear was back. "Is this some kind of joke?"

"What? No!" I took a step toward her but stopped when she backed away. "I got that audition slot for you. I wasn't going to get into Juilliard over you. It was never about me."

Bianca laughed and I hated her for it.

Collette's blush deepened. "Don't you see why this was all about you? You never asked me. You just acted." Her arms wrapped around her stomach as she turned away from me. She was slipping from my grasp and I was desperate to hold onto her.

"But you deserve to be seen," I said. "Your talent deserves to be seen."

Collette was blinking rapidly, her breath was coming out in shallow gasps that had me worried. "But that's just it. It's my decision. Not yours."

"I know, but I thought..." Oh crap, all of my reasoning flew out the window. My epic grand plan was looking more and more like an epic fail. "I wanted to be by your side," I said. "I thought we could both perform. Together."

By the confused way Collette was staring at me, one would think I'd just starting babbling in Chinese. "But don't you realize why this is even more insulting? My own mother was more willing to say yes to a guitarist instead of a dancer. It wasn't my merit that got me an audition. It was you and your...connections."

I hated the way she spoke about me and my family. Even though there was truth to it, the way she framed it made me feel slimy. Dirty. Like I was no better than my own father. "That wasn't my intention. I just knew you wouldn't stand up for yourself so I—"

"Go." Her voice was cold and harsh. I barely recognized it, but the one word seemed to ricochet off the walls and reverberate in the air around us.

No one spoke, no one moved. Not even Bianca.

"Collette, please," I started.

Collette turned away. "Just go away, Ethan. I don't want to see you right now."

I stared at her, my mouth still open as I tried to come up with something to say to make this right.

Nothing. I couldn't think of anything.

Her shoulders were hunched as she picked up her discarded hoodie, her back still to me.

"I'll call you," I said.

She never responded, not even as I walked out the door.

FOURTEEN

COLLETTE

Shock. I was definitely in a state of shock. That had to be why my heart was pounding like this—like it wanted to escape. That had to be why I could hear my own breath and why it was coming too quick, like I was about to hyperventilate or—

"I swear, Collette, if you throw up on the dance floor, I will kill you."

I whipped around to face Bianca. I'd almost forgotten she was there. I'd thought maybe she'd have left when Ethan did, but nope. There she stood in all her tall, slim glory looking like the evil harbinger of doom that she was.

"What are you still doing here?" I snapped.

Couldn't a girl wallow in private? Tears were already threatening and I needed to make sense of everything that had just happened. Everything he'd said.

He expected me to dance. In public. For Juilliard.

In front of my mother.

Was he *insane*?

I should have clued him in on the state of the studio but after our chat, Mom swore me to secrecy and I had no problem keeping it quiet. There was no need to panic all the dancers. Especially since Juilliard was going to pick someone from our studio and the donors would start taking us seriously again.

Going against my wishes and signing me up for a slot didn't help my resolve to put dancing in the past. But neither did dancing with Ethan until all the walls I'd built up came crashing down.

I was still so confused by everything that was happening and everything I felt that I needed to sit down. Or a good ole' slap across the face to wake me up.

"Seriously, have you lost your mind?" Bianca said. I had a feeling she'd been talking nonstop for a while now and I was only now tuning in. "What were you guys even doing in here?"

I shook my head, gathering up my stuff so I could go back to my house, away from Bianca, and away from this space. The studio used to bring me so much happiness, but now? It held too many memories. My breathing grew even faster as I remembered the way Ethan held me. The way he'd touched me. The way he'd made me feel so exquisitely beautiful, so...so *perfect*.

For a second there I'd actually felt like I was perfect. Like I was beautiful and graceful and like...

Like a freakin' princess in a fairytale.

That's exactly what it had been. A fairytale.

All it took was one look for me to throw my resolve out the window. I was weak and I hated that I felt that way.

"So?" Bianca's voice was insistent. She had the kind of personality that refused to be ignored. If she wasn't the center of attention, her world would implode. Right now there'd be no getting away from here without giving her what she wanted.

"What?" I snapped, my bag over my shoulder as I got ready to flee. "What do you want to know? Was I dancing?" I slapped a hand over my chest as I feigned shock. "Yes. I, Collette Boucher, actually had the nerve to dance. For fun. In private." I gave her what I hoped was a withering stare as I approached. "Now, can I leave?"

"Can you *run away*, you mean?" she taunted, not shifting from where she stood in the doorway, blocking my path. "I suppose. It's what you do best, right?"

I stopped in my tracks and stared at her. Anger was almost a relief compared to all the other emotions that were brewing under the surface.

Anger I understood. Anger was actionable.

Anger was so much better than hurt.

"You don't know anything about me, Bianca." My voice was little more than a growl.

She didn't look fazed. If anything, she seemed amused as she studied me. "Oh please. We've been going to school together for years. I know you." She glanced meaningfully toward the area where Ethan had been standing just moments ago. "I also know you're an idiot if you let that guy go."

I narrowed my eyes, clutching my bookbag strap as I tried to keep my cool. "Don't talk about Ethan," I said. "You have no idea—"

"That you two have been dancing together?" she finished. "Uh, yeah, that was pretty clear from that little Dirty Dancing routine I just caught."

I scowled. "It wasn't—"

"Whatever." She waved away my protest like it was an irritating gnat. "I don't really care what you two have been getting up to after dark, but don't insult my intelligence. There was enough steam in this room to open a spa."

I stared at her open-mouthed for a minute because...she was serious. She honestly thought there'd been something there.

Because there was.

I gave my head a little shake, blocking out the image of his head dipping down toward mine, his hands on my waist, that look in his eyes...

"Ugh, you people are the worst."

Bianca's words, muttered under her breath, had my focus back on her. She looked prissy as ever with her lips pursed and her perfect blonde hair gleaming in a long ponytail.

"*You people?*" I repeated.

She rolled her eyes, shoving away from the door frame to drop her own bag on the floor. "Non-dancers. Normal people. Muggles. Teenagers." She waved a hand. "Whatever you want to call yourself."

My anger was only briefly interrupted by surprise. "*You* know what muggles are?"

Her even gaze told me clearly that she thought I was an idiot. Or possibly that I was missing the point.

Everything else she said came to me in a rush and I found myself scowling in indignation. "I'm not a *non*-dancer."

Even when I'd stopped taking the advanced classes I'd still thought of myself as a dancer. I mean, I still went to the academy, and I still danced on my own time, and I still loved it with all my heart. That counted for something, right? "I *am* a dancer," I said, a little more forcefully.

She arched a brow in disbelief.

"I dance," I said. "Just..." I gestured around the room. "After hours."

"Mm-hmm." She turned away, and I got the feeling I'd been dismissed.

"Hey, I love dance just as much as you—"

"No." She whipped around so quickly I jerked back. She jabbed a finger in my direction. "There is no comparison to my training and whatever it is you're doing here with that guy when no one is watching."

I blinked in surprise at the rare show of emotion. Her

normally icy eyes flashed with anger and pink tinged her high cheekbones as she glared at me. "You were told by *one* teacher that you didn't have what it took—"

"That teacher was my mother," I felt compelled to point out.

She ignored that. "One teacher told you that you should quit...and you *did.*" Her pretty face turned ugly with a sneer. "Some of us deal with criticism and rejection on a daily basis and we don't quit. Some of us are *killing ourselves* trying to prove that—"

She cut herself off so abruptly, the silence seemed to echo with her unspoken rage.

I could only stare in disbelief, because of all the many faces of Bianca I'd seen—the brown-noser, the spoiled brat, the determined dancer—I'd never once seen her lose her cool like that.

But that glimpse of genuine emotions was over in the blink of an eye. She straightened her shoulders, took a deep breath, and—just like that—the angry teenage girl was gone, and she was once again in full control as she eyed me from head to toe with that judgemental smirk I knew way too well. "You might dance for fun," she said coolly. "But you'll never be a dancer."

I sucked in air to try and buffer the blow. I should be used to this already. For years I'd been hearing comments like this from her, and it was time to face it head on. "Right," I said, as matter-of-factly as I was able. "Because I look like this and you look like...you."

She turned to me with her brows drawn together like I'd just grown a second head. "What? No." She took a step toward me, her ponytail swinging over her shoulder. "You're not a dancer because you're not cut out for it."

"Exactly," I said. "I'm not built for it. You and my mother and everyone else has been telling me that for years. I get it."

"Clearly you don't," she snapped. "I didn't say you weren't

built for it. I said you weren't cut out for it. There's a difference."

I didn't want to listen to her. I didn't need to hear this, and yet...a little part of me was curious.

She sighed loudly, not trying to hide her exasperation. "Your body is...whatever. It's fine. But if you're going to quit at the first sign of an obstacle? Then clearly you're not cut out for the life of a dancer."

I stared at her. Was she saying what I thought she was saying? "*You* are saying that my body is 'fine.'" I'd used air quotes and she arched her brows as she looked at my hands in the air.

She shrugged. "Yeah, I mean it's not ideal, but people have made it in the dance world with worse handicaps than *hips*."

My mouth was definitely hanging open now. "You...you—" I drew in a deep breath and tried again. "You've been telling me I'm too fat for *years*."

Bianca shrugged. She *shrugged*. "So? Kids at my old school called me skeletor all of junior high, you don't hear me moaning about it."

I gaped at her but her expression was bland, like she honestly didn't get what the big deal was.

"You're cruel to me—"

"No, I'm honest with you," she said simply. Throughout all of this her voice never rose and her cheeks never flushed. She looked so unperturbed, so unflustered. It made me want to pull her hair until she screamed.

"People will call you fat," she said over her shoulder as she fiddled with the knobs on the stereo. "Especially in the ballet world which is crazy, I mean, let's face it, there will always be someone skinnier or better than you" She stood up and brushed her hands on her tights, like this was a commonplace in dance. She was prepared for it, why wasn't I?. "And some people will call me skinny, and they'll call Eve short and they'll call Tilly stupid and..." She threw her hands up in disgust. "What are you going to do? Run away every time your feelings get hurt?"

I blinked at that because I had no answer.

She seemed to know it, too, because she went over to her bag and started rustling through it like we were done and she was ready to move on.

Except we weren't. I wasn't close to being done. I felt like everything I thought about myself, my future, had already been set in stone. Hearing I could change fate—from Bianca, no less —was, unsettling.

"I don't—" I started, not even sure what I wanted to say. "I didn't mean to—"

She mercifully cut me off with a loud, exasperated sigh. "Do us both a favor and save the heart-to-hearts for your boyfriend."

"He's not my boyfriend," I said automatically. The moment I did, it all came rushing back. The sadness. The hurt. The confusion.

"Well, that's your own dumb fault." Yup, that was Bianca. Always the sweetheart.

I started to walk away. "It's not that simple." She didn't know everything, even if she believed otherwise. Sure, I could accept my weight with some work, but none of that mattered if the school was shut down.

But no matter how much I wanted to throw that in her face, I couldn't. I had to bite my tongue and just let her think the only issue standing between me and dancing was my weight.

"Uh huh," she muttered. "Whatever you say."

I should walk away. I should just leave and ignore her and—

"He could have anyone he wanted." I hated my stupid

mouth for blurting it out like that. As if Bianca didn't already think I was pathetic.

She turned slowly to face me, crossing her arms like she was settling in for another unwanted conversation. Everything about her demeanor was patronizing and annoying and...honest.

At least she was honest with me.

Olivia and Ethan—they saw what they wanted to see. They cared about me too much to give the harsh truth. And right now, that was what I wanted.

I pursed my lips and started again. "He can have any girl he wants—"

"But he wants you." She finished my sentence with a shrug. Like it was so obvious. Like it wasn't totally crazy.

I stared at her in silence for a moment until she arched her brows in obvious annoyance. "Are we done here? Some of us have to practice for auditions."

I left the studio so she could rehearse, but her words stuck with me.

But he wants you.

Did he?

The thought was terrifying, and I didn't know why. Maybe because I knew that if I let myself believe it...If I even let myself hope...

I'd be opening myself up to a world of hurt.

My dance with him, the way he'd held me, the things Bianca had said afterward...my head was reeling for the next few days. I half hoped that Ethan would text, and then I told myself it wouldn't fix anything if he did. Even if I had enough courage to dance because I was a dancer, it didn't change the status of the school.

FIFTEEN

ETHAN

To say I was miserable was an understatement. It was strange. I knew I should hate Collette for treating me that way. I knew I should hate Bianca for ruining our moment.

I knew I should hate my team for putting me in this situation in the first place.

But I didn't.

I was just...numb.

Ryan must have noticed my mood during lunch on Thursday because suddenly he shouldered me. Annoyance shot through me and I growled as I glanced over at him.

"What?" I barked.

He raised his eyebrows. "Whoa. What's with you?"

I shoved my tray away from me and leaned back against my chair and folded my arms. "Nothing."

He studied me like he didn't believe a word I said. I just shrugged as I finished off my Coke and crumpled the can with my hand. The jagged metal jabbed into my hand and made me feel something. I wasn't going to lie, it felt good.

"Whatever, man," Ryan said as he threw up his hands. "Are

you coming tonight or not? I don't want to deal with a prima donna and if you're going to be moody, don't come."

I cleared my throat as I glanced over at my friend. Sure, I was being a jerk. But I was hurting. In a way that I'd never hurt before. Losing Collette was one of the worst things to happen to me. Which just made me sound pathetic.

Maybe she was right. I did live a cushy life. The worst thing that happened to me was my dad not letting me play guitar. I was lame and Collette knew it. That's why she never called or texted after I left the studio on Monday.

And I didn't blame her. I wouldn't call me either.

I sighed and shrugged as I pushed around some crumbs on the table in front of me. "Sorry. I'm just...going through something."

Ryan fell silent and when I looked over at him, I saw a spark of sympathy.

"Your dad?" he asked.

If there was any of my friends who understood what it was like to have a rocky relationship with his father, it was Ryan. At least for me, my dad was still in the picture. Ryan's bounced in and out of his life like a ping pong ball that was hit too hard.

"Yeah, that and other things." I was always going to have a problem with my dad, but right now, my frustration with my father was the easier of my rocky emotions to understand.

"Ah," Ryan said, his typical, obnoxious demeanor returning. "That hottie from the dance school haunting your thoughts?" Then he leaned in and gave me a wicked smile. "Because she's haunting my dreams. I keep imagining her as the teacher and I'm the tardy student." He made an obnoxious whipping sound, completely oblivious to the fact that I was glaring at him.

Anger coursed through me as I imagined Collette being the star of his raunchy fantasies. "You dream about Collette?" I felt my hand fisting as it rested in my lap. He was my friend but I had no problem decking him.

Ryan furrowed his brow. "Who's Collette?" Then recognition passed over his face. "Oh, that chunky girl from the hallway? You have a thing for her?"

His words had me standing and towering over him. "Don't call her that."

Ryan's eyes widened. "Call her what? Chunky? Isn't that why she isn't allowed in that ridiculously prissy school?" Ryan raised his hands. "It's not a bad thing. She's hot too." His gaze landed on my fist and then back to my face.

"Calm down," Cooper said on my other side as he rested his hand on my shoulder.

I stared Ryan down but then realization passed over me. Punching my friend wasn't going to make me feel better. Punching Ryan wasn't going to bring Collette back.

So I growled, grabbed my backpack, and headed out of the lunch room.

Once I got to my locker, I punched the metal, allowing the feeling of pain to shoot up my arm. Then I sighed as I leaned against it and closed my eyes. I was an idiot if I thought fighting was the answer to my problems. If anything, it would just result with me in detention and an extra lecture about keeping up appearances from my dad.

And with the way I was feeling, anything my dad had to say would just tick me off more.

"Are you about done throwing a fit?" Ryan's voice piped up from behind me.

I opened my eyes and turned to see that he was approaching me cautiously. Feeling defeated, I shrugged and focused my attention on opening my locker. "What do you want?" I asked as I swung the door open and stared aimlessly inside.

When Ryan didn't speak right away, I peered over just to make sure he was still there. And he was, leaning against a nearby locker with his hands shoved into the front pockets of his jeans. His brow was furrowed as he studied me.

"You made a promise to me, dude. You told me you'd play with my band. I paid the deposit and everything. Where am I going to get someone else on such short notice?"

I sighed as the responsibility to help everyone else but myself settled on my shoulders. Ryan wanted me to stick it to my dad and play in his band. Coach Reynolds wanted me to be a better leader. Dad wanted me to be the perfect Morrison. And Collette? Well, she wanted everything but me.

My life sucked.

Also, I sucked because I'd been hemming and hawing over this stupid gig all week. I'd been avoiding giving Ryan a straightforward answer because I hoped...

Ah heck, I didn't know what I'd hoped. That my life would magically sort itself out? Life didn't work that way. "I wish I could but my dad set up this thing with a recruiter. I told him I had something else going on but...you know my dad. He's a loser." I shoved my hands through my hair and shrugged. Ryan snorted in a mocking way and it just made the heat under my collar burn hotter. I turned and glared at him.

"What?" I asked.

Ryan didn't flinch. Instead, he straightened and met my gaze with as much stubbornness as I was dishing out.

"You're the reason your life sucks, dude," he said as he reached out and shoved my shoulder.

I glared at him. He had no idea why my life sucked. "Just leave me alone," I said as I turned to face my locker.

"Why? Man, I'm so sick of your martyr act. You seriously have every opportunity laid out in front of you." He raised his voice in a mocking manner as he grasped his hands and placed them next to his cheek. "I'm Ethan. My dad wants me to go to Yale and I not only have the grades for it, but the money as well. I'm the quarterback of the football team and a hot ballerina wants me. I have ridiculous talent when it comes to music but my life still sucks." He blinked his eyelashes a few times.

And I wanted to punch him.

"That's how you see me?" I asked.

Ryan straightened and cleared his throat as a sophomore walked past, eyeing him like he was crazy. He shot her a smile and then glanced back at me. "Pretty much. You'd get everything you want if you'd just stand up for yourself. Life is hard. No need to make it worse by putting limitations on yourself."

He shifted and pulled his backpack strap up higher on his shoulder. "It's pathetic and lame." Then his expression turned serious. "And my friend, Ethan? He's not pathetic and lame."

I stared at him. I hated it, but he was right. Not wanting to admit it, I turned to my locker and focused my attention on the few books I had lined up on the top shelf. So many thoughts were swirling around in my mind and yet I had no idea how I was going to say any of them.

Ryan was right, my problems started and ended with me. If I wanted a different life, I needed to be forward about it. Even if that meant disappointing my dad.

The bell rang and Ryan sighed as he shifted his weight.

"I really hope to see you tonight. I'll keep a mic open for you. But if not, I get it as well. My life will go on." His hand landed on my shoulder. "Just know that I don't think you're a wuss like your dad does. You're so much more than a junior senator to his president."

He squeezed my shoulder and left.

I stood in front of my locker, a turmoil of emotions crashing into me as I tried to process what I was going to do.

Truth was, I was sick of living in my father's shadow. I was tired of trying to live up to his expectations. But what did I know about my future? How did I know if my plans were really what I wanted?

How does anyone know?

Maybe it had just been easy, following the path my parents wanted. At least then, I didn't have to worry about failing. They were a safety net that I was used to having and the idea of jumping without the knowledge that they were there scared me.

More than I wanted to admit.

I guess Collette and I had more in common than I thought. My parents and their plans for me were my own personal hoodie. If I truly cared about Collette, I'd take my own advice. I'd get over the stupid insecurities that were holding me back and I'd be the man *I* wanted to be.

I'd be the man Collette deserved.

MY HEART POUNDED as I slipped into my parents' room that afternoon. I wasn't normally a ninja, but right now, I didn't want to face my father and his disappointment. But I also didn't want to lose Yale and my potential to go there.

Sure, I'd decided that I didn't want my parents to dictate my life but I also didn't want to throw my future away. Being a rock star really didn't pay like being a lawyer did. And I wasn't naïve to think I had enough talent or musical ambition to make it big.

Truth was, I wasn't sure what I wanted for my future, other than Collette. I guess I just wanted the chance to figure it out for myself. College was the ideal place to do that, and a great university would offer every opportunity I could imagine.

So I settled with the next best thing. Sneaking around

behind my parents' backs. There was a chance I could still meet with the recruiter *and* play in Ryan's band. If my plan worked.

My parents' room was still and pristine. I felt like I was walking into a hospital room with how white and shiny all their surfaces were. My parents took appearance seriously—even into their bedroom.

I rolled my eyes as I tiptoed over to my dad's desk and began to riffle through his papers on it. Bills. Proposals. Emails.

All of it was boring stuff. Not at all what I needed.

I turned my back on the door and focused on the bulletin board above Dad's computer. I was looking for the recruiter's number or information. Any way of getting a hold of him. Or her. I wasn't really sure.

"What are you doing?" Chrissy's voice made me jump.

I knocked over a container full of pens as I whipped around. Wincing, I scrambled to keep them from falling on the ground. "Geez, Chris," I said as I glared at her.

She giggled as she walked over and helped me clean up. "What are you doing?" she asked again.

When we finished putting everything back in place, she straightened and folded her arms. I knew that look. She wasn't going anywhere.

I sighed as I turned my attention back to searching. "I'm looking for something." I hoped that would appease her, but it didn't and when I glanced over at her, I saw her raised eyebrows and her finger tapping her forearm.

"Okay," I responded. "I'm looking for the contact info of the Yale recruiter."

"Why?"

"I want to invite them to something." I shot her a pleading look. "Can you help me?"

She narrowed her eyes. "If you tell me what the something is, I'll tell you what I know."

I scoffed. I did *not* appreciate the shakedown my little sister was giving me. But on the other hand, I was proud of her tenacity. "Ryan wants me to play with his band tonight. If I invite the recruiter as well, two birds, one stone."

She furrowed her brow. "There are birds in the band?"

"What? No. It's just a saying."

She snorted. "Yeah, an old saying." Then she stepped forward and lifted the corners of the paper and let them fall. "I fulfilled my end of the bargain. Now it's your turn."

She studied me and then nodded. "Well, I don't know his number but I know his name. Will that help?"

I pulled out my phone as my heart began to pound. I found my search tab and pressed it so the cursor was ready. "Yeah, that will work. What's his name?"

Chrissy sighed. "But Dad is going to freak, Ethan."

I held her shoulders and bent my knees so I could look her straight in the eyes. "I'll deal with Dad. I'll explain everything to him later."

She bit her lip. "When?"

I squeezed her shoulders. "When it's too late for him to stop me."

Her tension faded with a grin. "Boris Blakely."

I nodded as I typed his name. Then I added "Yale" at the end and a few seconds later, I found his information on the school website. I glanced up at the clock and saw that it was only two o'clock. I still had a chance of catching him before he left. Or at least his receptionist would know how to get a hold of him.

As the phone started to ring, I moved toward Chrissy and waved her out. I couldn't wait to get to the safety of being anywhere but snooping around in my parents' room.

As soon as I'd latched the door to my bedroom the ringing stopped and a high pitched and preppy voice asked, "Mr. Blakely's office. How can I help you?"

I closed my eyes as I pumped a fist in the air. I was finally taking control of my future and it felt great. I could have my cake and eat it too.

Just watch.

SIXTEEN

COLLETTE

Three days later and...let's face it. I was a wreck.

Olivia pried out every detail about me and Ethan on Monday night, but she was no help. She thought I was crazy to be so angry about what Ethan had done and even crazier to listen to anything Bianca had said. The only thing she'd agreed on was that Ethan wanted me...as more than a friend.

On Thursday Olivia came to our house after school so we could get ready for the Morrison hosted fundraiser. My mom had insisted that I come along and no amount of pleading and badgering could get me out of it. And from her stressed expression, I didn't want to add more to her plate.

She had, at least, let me invite Olivia along as well. At least I'd have moral support.

"Come on, wuss, let's go in there so you can tell Ethan how sorry you are."

I frowned over at her as she shoved me toward the front doors of the fancypants country club where the fundraiser was being held. "I'm not a wuss," I said.

"Whatever you say, chicken."

My moral support was a big believer in tough love. Especially these last few days when she'd become Ethan's biggest champion.

I paused just inside the doors, my gaze sweeping across the room for any sign of him as my mother went on ahead, calling out to Mr. Lewis, a friend of hers from the academy's board of trustees. I eyed them, wondering if there had been any progress on the 'closing the academy' front.

"Eww," Olivia said.

I glanced over at her. "What?"

"Please don't tell me you're moving on with *him*." She pointed to Mr. Lewis.

My cheeks heated. "What? No. That's just...I'm..." Nothing I could say could keep my mom's secret so I just shrugged and began to scan the crowd. "I don't see Ethan," I said.

Olivia seemed to have moved on from the idea of me and Mr. Lewis and our May-December romance. "Are you going to run away when you do?" She arched her brows. "Tell me now so I'm prepared to tackle you before you hit the door."

I frowned over at her. "Very funny."

She shrugged. "I'm just sayin'..."

I knew what she was 'just sayin'—she'd been saying it for days now. I didn't want to go down this road again—not here, and not now when I'd run into him at any moment. And yet, despite my intentions, I found myself arguing with her for the millionth time.

"He had no right to make that decision for me!"

Olivia sighed. I imagined she was just as tired of this conversation as I was.

She thought I was nuts to still be so angry, but she just didn't get it. He should have understood better than anyone how hard it was to take a chance on a dream. And he should have taken my word for it when I said I wouldn't be a dancer—that I couldn't.

You're not cut out for it.

I winced. Days later and I was still wincing over some of the things Bianca had said.

Maybe because they were the truth. Maybe I should have fought harder, or dieted more, or opted for surgery to make my body into the kind that would fit my mother's ideal.

I closed my eyes and took a deep breath. Now was not the time to rehash all that. This wasn't about me, or my mother, it was about Ethan and his heavy-handed interfering.

"Why would he do that?" I asked, as if this time Olivia might have the magic answer.

She gave me a droll look. "I don't know, Collette. Maybe if you'd given him a chance to explain, you'd have your answers."

I bit my lip, thoroughly chastised. Again. She was right. I knew she was right. I needed to talk to him. I at least needed to hear what he had to say for himself.

I took a deep breath and summoned my courage. "Where is Ethan?"

I'd asked it under my breath so I was more than a little startled when a child's voice beside me answered.

"You're a friend of Ethan's?"

I turned to find a cute little girl with a huge welcoming smile.

"Uh, yeah, you could say that."

"I'm Chrissy, his sister."

Before I could say 'nice to meet you' she was leaning into me, her voice the loudest whisper I'd ever heard. "Ethan's not here because he's playing with a band!"

I blinked at her as Olivia smothered a laugh. "Well, look who grew a pair," she said under her breath.

I was too busy blinking like an idiot to respond.

He'd done it. Ethan Morrison had actually done it. "He's... he's playing at The Tailgate tonight?"

Chrissy nodded eagerly, but before she could reply, her father came over. "Christina, have you seen your brother?"

I blinked at the older man in shock. I'd seen him before—I'd stood a few feet away from him the other night at the stadium—but I'd never stood face to face with him like this. I'd never really *looked* at him.

He looked just like Ethan. You know, if Ethan were a couple decades older and walked around like he owned the world.

"Dad, this is Ethan's friend," Chrissy started the introductions.

He flashed me a smile that was as fake as they come, not bothering to ask my name. "How do you do?" He turned back to Chrissy. "Where's Ethan?"

She shrugged.

I'll just come right out and say it. I wouldn't want to be on Chrissy's bad side. She lied like a professional poker player and her voice was sickeningly sweet as she said, "I don't know, Daddy. I haven't seen him."

I stared at her in shock. Olivia's expression was one of awe. I was pretty sure Olivia had just found her new spirit animal and its name was Chrissy.

Ethan's mother joined them a second later. "He's not coming."

It was eerie the way she managed to hiss this so Ethan's dad could hear while never faltering with that creepy plastic smile.

"What do you mean, he's not coming?" Again with the creepy fake smiling.

Ethan's mother held up her phone. "The recruiter's secretary left me a voicemail confirming Ethan's meeting." Her botoxed forehead didn't budge, but I saw the confusion in her eyes as she added, "Some place called The Tailgate?"

Olivia and I turned to one another.

"What is going on?" she whispered.

I shrugged and shook my head. I had no idea, but I was excited. I had no other word for it. My heart was racing at the thought of Ethan performing live.

My head was still saying 'we're mad at him' but my heart was tripping over itself in anticipation. "I have to be there."

It was like a universal law or something. There was no debate, just a fact. If Ethan Morrison was going to play live, I had to be there.

The need to be there—now—was overwhelming. My eyes widened and Olivia grabbed my arm, clearly seeing my desperation. "Come on, we'll find a ride."

My mom was lost in the crowd. She wouldn't leave to go drop me off at a club, anyway. We looked for anyone else we knew, and then...

"Oh no," I sighed.

"Oh yes." Olivia took me over to the bar area where a bored-looking Bianca was standing, tapping at her phone while some guy who looked just as bored looked on, holding two glasses of club soda, by the looks of it.

"Bianca," Olivia said. "We need you."

She lifted her head slowly. "Since when do they allow just anyone at these events?"

Olivia opened her mouth to reply, but I beat her to it. "Please."

They both turned to look at me. Slowly. Like maybe they'd misheard. "What did you say?"

I huffed. "Come on, Bianca. I know you don't like me and I don't like you and you don't like Olivia and Olivia doesn't like anyone and blah blah blah..." I paused to inhale. "But I need your help and despite what you'd have everyone believe, I am almost twenty percent positive that somewhere within that skeletor ribcage, you have a heart."

The silence that followed was deafening.

"Whoa." The bored blond guy broke it with that eloquent rejoinder.

"Wow," Olivia muttered.

Bianca slipped her phone in her clutch. "Fine. It beats standing around with bozo here."

And that was how the three of us—blond guy opted to stay behind—ended up at The Tailgate just in time to see Ryan's band go onstage.

"Ew, this is *his* band?" Bianca whined as we made our way through the crowd to the edge of the stage.

"I told you we were coming here to see Ethan," I snapped.

"That's not what I—" She sighed. "Forget it."

Already forgotten. I was tugging both her and Olivia along behind me in my eagerness to get close. I didn't want to miss anything. Not. A. Thing.

The guys were tuning their guitars, Ryan was doing a mic check.

It was so freakin' legit. I wondered if Ethan's heart was beating just as hard as mine was.

"This is incredible," Olivia squealed beside me as she shook my arm.

Bianca did not squeal but her lack of whining spoke for itself. She was impressed—just a little.

"Hey look, it's the prom queen and her court!" Some drunken buffoon pointed to us and laughed. Olivia sneered but I was looking up at the stage and saw Ethan's head lift. I ducked down behind Olivia and just as he scanned the crowd.

"What are you doing?" Olivia asked as she moved in a circle to get away from me.

I shot her a pleading look but it was too late. My gaze shifted over to Ethan and I watched as his eyes darkened the moment they landed on me.

And just like that, the last three days flew out the window. We might as well have been *there*—back in our studio. He might as well still have been holding me in his arms. I was just as breathless, my head just as fuzzy, my heartbeat just as frantic.

Ethan's brow furrowed as he studied me. He parted his lips but before he could ask whatever he wanted to ask, his gaze shifted to Ryan who was strumming a few chords.

"*One, two, three, four!*" Ryan's low voice boomed over the crowd and they were off. The music pulsing, pounding—so not at all like the beautiful, soft melodies Ethan played for me in our private sessions.

And the look on Ethan's face as he played along was nothing like I'd ever seen before. He talked about me and how amazing I was when I danced. But watching Ethan play only solidified what I'd known all along.

He was born to play.

The music was primal and pulsing. It was bass-driven, the throbbing tempo and thrumming chords filled the entire room. It rocketed through me and I couldn't *not* move along with the music. It wasn't even intentional, my muscles were working in time with the beat, the notes and the energy like a live wire in this room, making me and everyone around me dance like puppets.

This was dancing...and it wasn't. It was everything I loved about the way the music filled you, spoke to you, was transformed by you, and then came back into the world in the form of liquid movement.

My mind went blank. Blissfully blank. I reveled in the feel that was at once totally familiar and utterly unique. It was the same sensation that I got while dancing in the studio but a million times more intense.

My movements felt frantic as my body kept pace with the bass, my arms moving over my head as my eyes—well my eyes never moved.

My body was at the mercy of this music, but my gaze was fixed on Ethan. I'd always loved to watch him play, but this... this was something else entirely.

He was beautiful.

Was that a weird thing to think about a guy? Maybe. But it was true. He was as handsome as ever but there was an intensity about him that few got to see. That few were ever lucky enough to witness.

I felt Olivia's movements beside me and, yes, even Bianca was swept up in it. I couldn't see them, but I felt them, and it was the craziest thing that after dancing together for years, this was the very first time I'd ever actually felt like I was dancing *with* them.

I heard Olivia's laughter followed by a *whoop*, as she threw her hands up in the air after the first song ended. Even Bianca was clapping on my other side. Ethan grinned and his smile that I loved so much was aimed at me.

Only me.

My heart was lodged somewhere in my throat because there were so many things I wanted to say to him in that moment. So many things that were desperate to come out. I couldn't hold them in any longer.

Olivia leaned forward. "Uh...is he staring at you?"

I jerked my eyes away from Ethan, oddly flustered that we'd been caught having an intimate moment in the middle of a crowded club. But she wasn't looking at me, she was talking to Bianca.

Bianca who basically snarled in response. "Don't be stupid."

I looked to Olivia who was looking at the stage, where Ryan was, in fact, staring at Bianca.

I looked over at her too but now her chin was tilted high and she was pretending to ignore us.

Interesting.

The music started up again, and I forgot all about Bianca and Ryan and even Olivia, because Ethan was mesmerizing up there. He really was.

Olivia leaned over again. "When's the last time you had this much fun dancing?" she shouted over the music.

I shook my head. I couldn't remember.

"Never," Bianca said on my other side. Her tone brooked no arguments. And maybe she was right. Maybe this was the first time any of us had danced just for fun.

I let the music sweep me away again, my limbs loose and my hips moving in a way that would have made the Juilliard people faint. This time I shut my eyes and I let myself go. I abandoned myself to the beauty of it all—the sweaty, frantic, glorious beauty of it all.

"Get 'em up there!" It was that same drunken moron again, and for a second I was confused when I felt arms around me and suddenly I was flat on my back and airborne. And then it happened so fast. Hands were all over my body as the sea of people carried me to the stage. I shot Olivia a panicked look, but she was just beaming as she cheered on the people who were touching us.

For a girl who always felt too heavy, I was freakin' weightless in the air. One second, maybe two—to me it felt like an eternity before my feet were set on the ground and when I stood upright—I was on the stage.

In the spotlight.

"Yeah, girl!" Olivia screamed.

Bianca was shouting. Why was Bianca shouting? "Dance!" I read her lips more than heard it because the crowd was loud and the instruments behind me were deafening.

I whipped around to see Ethan grinning at me. "Ready?" he mouthed it the same way I had before I'd launched myself into his arms. The night I broke his heart.

My heart stopped beating at the memory. He wanted me to let go. Surrender. Trust that he and the other guys in the band had my back. They'd hold me up.

I shut my eyes. I took a deep breath. And I did it...I let go.

Here, on stage, I didn't have the weight of the world on my shoulders. I didn't have to worry about the studio or how my mother's heart would be crushed if it closed.

For now, I could have fun. I'd deal with reality when the music stopped.

For now, I'd be a dancer.

SEVENTEEN

ETHAN

Collette was so beautiful, it almost hurt to watch her.

I'd seen glimpses of this side of her in the studio. I'd caught flashes of this young woman who was so lost in the music she forgot to be afraid; a girl so vulnerable and confident, she could conquer the world.

But here, tonight...it was more than a glimpse and it lasted so much longer than a flash. For a little while there as I played and she danced, I fooled myself into thinking it would never end.

I didn't know why she was here or what this meant but for as long as she danced and I played, only one thing mattered.

She came.

Collette was *here* and she was too stunning for words. Only music and dance would do. In that short black dress, with her hair pulled up, she was elegance personified. Yet, dancing like she was, with utter abandon, she was joyful and unrestrained. Wild and chaotic and graceful, all at once.

Maybe this was why her mother feared she wouldn't fit into

the world of ballet. She could master form and technique, but beneath all that she was genuine and unrestrained.

When the last song ended, I watched her come back from that place she went when she danced. I imagined it was the same place I went when I played music—that place where I felt weightless and free. Her dreamy expression faded as she blinked a few times like she was readjusting to this world with its limitations and the full force of its gravity.

She gave me a small, sad smile, before turning to leave the stage. I reached out and stopped her with a hand on her arm. "Wait for me to finish," I whispered. "Please."

She hesitated but then she nodded and slipped off the stage with the help of Olivia and Bianca.

Offstage was a madhouse as we rushed to remove our gear so the next band could set up. "We did it, man," Ryan shouted, clapping me on the shoulder as he passed. He was practically humming with excitement and a post-show adrenaline buzz. "You didn't let us down."

My chest swelled with pride. I still had to deal with my father but there was no doubt in my mind that the choices I'd made today were the right ones. I'd chosen my friend, I'd chosen to strike my own path...I'd chosen *myself*.

Ryan and I weren't exactly big on touchy-feely moments, though, so I didn't say any of that. I just smirked. "Was there ever any doubt?"

Ryan laughed as he shook his head. "Nah, man, of course not." He nodded toward the audience. "Go on, get out there and see your girl. We can take it from here."

He didn't have to tell me twice. I headed off to find Collette, shouting my thanks as I went. I was desperate to see her again, to talk to her. I knew I needed to explain everything. I needed to make this right. She was probably still angry, maybe even scared. But the fact that she'd come here tonight to see me...that had to count for something, right?

"You were amazing up there." I heard her before I saw her.

Whipping around I found her grinning at me, her eyes filled with pride and joy, along with a million other emotions. She looked nervous, and weary, and shy—well, shy for Collette.

Pretty much exactly how I felt.

But I was excited, too, and more than a little hopeful because...*she came.*

I took a step closer, noting distantly that Olivia and Bianca stood a few feet away, unabashedly watching us but not close enough to eavesdrop.

I took a step closer so we could hear each other over the surrounding crowd without shouting. "You were pretty incredible yourself."

Her gaze flickered up to the stage and I caught a hint of that dreaminess again, but it was tempered by something else. Something bittersweet.

"I can't believe you did it," Collette said, her voice filled with awe. "I can't believe you chose music over Yale."

"I didn't," I said quickly. "Or at least, I hope I didn't. I invited the recruiter here to watch me play. I thought maybe I could sell him on the fact that I'm more than football and good grades. I thought maybe he'd understand and...I don't know. Maybe it's wrong not to choose between the two but—"

"It's not wrong," she interrupted. "It's smart."

I met her gaze head-on to see if she was being honest. But this was Collette, of course she was being honest. She was never anything less than honest with me, and she deserved the same. "I'm going to tell my dad," I said.

Her lips hitched up in a cute little smile. "After tonight, I'd say you have to."

I nodded. The thought wasn't nearly as terrifying as it had

once been. Making the decision to choose my own dreams over my father's had been the hardest part. Now I was just seeing through what I'd started.

My father had been texting me all night asking me where I was and what I'd done. I planned to tell him on my own terms, just like I'd been hoping to explain everything to Collette in my own words on Monday before Bianca beat me to it. The thought made me desperate to explain now. The fact that she might still think I'd been somehow using her or been out to sabotage her...I couldn't let it lie. "I'd prepared a speech."

Of course, it probably would have helped if I hadn't blurted out the first words that popped into my head either.

Collette's eyes were wide with surprise. "Excuse me?"

I drew in a deep breath. "The other day," I said, clearing my throat and starting at the beginning. "At the studio, I'd had a speech prepared but Bianca beat me to it. I know what you think and—"

"You can't know what I think," she interrupted. With a helpless shrug, she added, "How can you know what I think when I don't even know myself?"

I nodded. "Fair enough. But that's why I want to explain."

Her lips twitched like she might say something, but she ended up nodding instead.

"I never set out to hurt you," I started. "When you walked away from me, after our kiss, I thought that I needed to show you how much I believe in you, how I see you..."

Her eyes widened slightly at that.

"I wanted to show how I felt," I said. "How I *feel*."

She took a deep breath but she still didn't speak.

"I wanted to show you that I could be the guy you wanted me to be. I could be strong and stand up to my father, and that we could go after our dreams together."

Her eyes grew wide and alarmingly shiny even in the dark lighting of this club. I cursed myself for not finding a place more private, but I was tired of waiting. Tired of not speaking when I had the chance and tired of not going after what I wanted.

"I care about you as a friend, Collette, but I want to be more. I like you more than that, and I—" My throat temporarily froze at the sight of tears in her eyes. "I hope you feel the same about me, too."

She didn't answer but her big blue eyes held a world of emotions and that alone gave me hope. She wasn't apathetic. She wasn't running away in horror. Deep down I had to believe she felt it too, and right now I needed to have faith in that to do what I needed to do.

"I asked your mother for an audition slot for you, Collette. For *us*."

Her watery eyes met mine evenly but her trembling lower lip gave away the intensity of her emotions.

"I wanted to surprise you with the chance for us to perform together. I wanted to give you the opportunity to seize your dreams. And I'd hoped I could be at your side when you did it. I thought if we both showed our parents what we're really about, maybe it would be easier." I reached out and grasped her hands in mine, and squeezed. "I wanted to show you how much I believe in you."

Even in this loud club, I heard her catch her breath.

"But..." I started.

I sighed as a tear spilled over and trickled down her cheek with that 'but.'

I swallowed, summoning the courage to do what needed to be done for her sake as well as mine. I couldn't make this choice for her. I couldn't make her choose herself or believe in herself...and I definitely couldn't force her to love herself.

The best I could do was give her the choice and let her decide.

"But," I said again, slower this time. "I realized something, Collette. I can't force you into being brave, and I can't make you see yourself the way that I do." I took a deep breath and forced out the words, hating the fact that they might hurt her. "I want to be with you, Collette. And I hope that you want me, too. But I've realized now that you'll never be able to trust me if you don't trust yourself." My heart ached as I steeled myself against her tears. "You'll never be able to believe that I love you unless you learn to love yourself."

She caught her lower lip in her teeth, but I heard the sob she'd tried to stifle.

I pulled her close, hoping to comfort her even though I knew it was me...*I* was the one who was hurting her. I wrapped my arms around her waist and dipped my head, blocking out the scene around us. "I still believe in you, and I'd be honored to be the one at your side when you're ready to face your fears."

She sniffed quietly, tears streaming down her face as she stared straight ahead, as if the buttons of my shirt might hold all the answers. I needed her to look at me, to know how serious I was...about her and about us.

I slipped my hand under her chin and tipped her face upward. She hesitated at first, but then allowed me to guide her gaze. I slid my fingers to her cheek so I could wipe away the tears that lingered there.

I reveled in the feeling of her skin against mine. There was so much I wanted to tell her. I wanted to show her just what she meant to me. I felt as if I would burst with emotions.

But I'd already talked too much this evening. I needed to act.

Before either of us could speak, I dipped down and kissed her softly. Her lips were warm and familiar. My whole body heated from her touch. She hesitated for a second but then she parted her lips and kissed me back. She moved closer to me and I responded by pulling her to my chest.

I could feel her hesitation. It cloaked what I knew was hidden deep inside of her. I knew there was a whole other level of passion she was suppressing. I could see it when she danced. She wasn't just jokes and quippy lines. She was elegance and perfection. If only I could draw that part of her out. If only I could make her feel comfortable enough around me to show that part.

For a second I felt like I could feel her heartbeat. She put everything that was holding her back into that kiss and I felt it all—her confusion, her desperation, her wanting to believe.

And as much as I wanted to confirm to her that she would find all of that in my kiss, I knew better. I didn't hold the answers she was seeking. I would always believe in her—but she needed to believe in herself.

She pulled back first and when she did, she shut her eyes rather than meet my gaze. I could all but feel her pulling away from me, shutting down.

She needed to think. She needed time.

I dropped my arms from around her waist and took a step back. "I'll be at the auditions tomorrow," I said.

Her head whipped up and her eyes snapped open. "What?"

"I'll be there tomorrow," I said again, hating the fear that was back in her eyes.

"I asked your mother for the slot and I'm not going to bail," I said. "And I plan on inviting my parents, for the record."

Her eyes widened and I wanted to reach for her again. But I didn't. I cared about her so much but I was starting to understand that the best way I could help her was to let her make this decision on her own.

Let her choose if she wanted to follow her dreams, if she wanted to choose herself...if she wanted to choose *me*.

"I can't make you go," I said. "And if you don't show, I'll play my music and make the best of it."

She was nibbling on her lip again, her eyes a watery mix of confusion and heartache and...and wanting.

She wanted to dance.

"I'll be there at your side," I said.

She stared at me for so long that the chords from the next band started up, the sounds of their off-key strumming as they warmed up broke through the silence and made her blink.

I saw it, the moment she made up her mind. She blinked once and then she shook her head. "I can't, Ethan, I'm sorry." She started to back away with another shake of her head. "I won't be there."

She turned and ran, lost in the crowd in seconds.

My heart seemed to go with her and I was left standing there, hollow. Empty.

She wasn't just choosing to walk away from auditions, she was choosing to walk away from me. She was choosing her fears and her insecurities rather than take a risk with me.

I tried to swallow down the pain, thrusting my hands into my pockets. Maybe she'd come around. Maybe she'd learn to see her own beauty and maybe she'd get over these issues that were holding her back and keeping me at arm's length. Maybe—

"There you are." The recruiter who I'd met just before the show was suddenly standing right next to me. "I thought you'd left before we could talk."

I faked a smile and reached out to shake his proffered hand.

Luckily he led the conversation because I was spent. I managed to say all of the right responses, but my heart wasn't into it. I barely managed to keep a smile on my face, not even when he said how impressed he was and told me how much he enjoyed seeing this side of a candidate—something real that didn't show up on the transcripts.

I should have been happy. He was impressed, the plan seemingly worked. I hadn't ruined my chances for the Ivy League, and I'd managed to live out a dream and help a friend.

As much as I tried to tell myself that the night had been a success, I wasn't convinced. None of it seemed to matter. Collette had walked away.

She'd heard my offer—the big grand gesture to come clean to the world about who we were and what we wanted. She'd heard it and she'd left.

By the time I got home, all I could think about was the look in her eyes before she'd run. The sadness, the pain, but mostly... the resignation. Like she was giving up.

That was what made it so hard to hope. I had this deep, unsettling sensation that she'd given up—on herself, on her dreams, and on us.

What else mattered now that the girl I loved had walked away?

Maybe that was why I barely flinched when I got home and ran right into a red-faced, thunderingly loud Dad. "What did you think you were doing?" he roared.

Chrissy must have been upstairs in bed—not asleep, no one could have slept with my father shouting like this. My mother sat quietly on the opposite side of the room, her lips pinched and the area around her eyes tight with tension.

"You embarrassed me tonight," my father said as I dropped my guitar case next to the stairs. "You had no right to contact that recruiter—"

"Actually, Dad, I had every right." I spoke quietly. I refused to match my father's anger. I didn't want to be like him and it would be a slippery slope if I ever let him pull me down to his level. "It's my future," I said calmly. "So that makes it my right."

My dad sputtered a bit—he wasn't used to me fighting back.

But I wasn't fighting. I was just finally standing up for myself. I was finally speaking the truth. "I'm sorry I wasn't there for your fundraiser," I said. "I try my best to help with the campaign stuff, but this time I'd made a commitment and you raised me to be the kind of man who honors his commitments."

He was staring at me like I'd sprouted a second head while my mother's eyes went comically wide.

"You raised me to be a leader, Dad." I met his gaze head-on as I walked toward him. "That means it's time for me to lead." I crossed my arms. "It's time for me to make my own decisions, and to plan my own future." I looked from him to my mom and back again. "Because that's the kind of man you've raised me to be."

Any other time I might have laughed at the way my dad's mouth flapped open and shut. I'd never once seen him at a loss for words, and the sight would have been hilarious if I could feel anything.

As it was, I was weary and exhausted. I had a feeling that sensation was a relief compared to what I'd feel when it finally sank in that Collette didn't choose me. That she might never choose me.

I turned and headed toward the staircase when it became clear that my parents were too stunned by my new attitude to form coherent words. I was exhausted and beat and I needed a hot shower and my bed.

I'd reached the bottom of the staircase when my dad finally managed. "Since when do you play in a band?"

I stopped. I turned. This, at least, was a valid question. "I don't," I said. "Not really. But I've been playing guitar for years."

"You have?" My mother sounded so confused I almost felt sorry for her.

"I have." I let out a sigh as I faced them fully. "I'm actually pretty good, too. The recruiter was impressed."

"The recruiter." My father's face started to turn red which meant that I was done here. "I can't believe you went behind our backs—"

"I wouldn't have had to if you'd ever listened to me," I said. "I wouldn't have had to sneak around if you'd ever once stopped and asked me what I wanted."

Honestly, you'd have thought I'd just told them that Martians had invaded.

"All I've ever worried about is your future," my father started.

"Yeah, the future you want for me," I said. "But that's not my future, that's your dream."

"Now listen here," he started, his voice booming once more as he fought to find his footing through his usual anger. "I've only ever acted out of your best interests and—"

"Here's the thing, Dad," I interrupted. Maybe it was the lack of emotions that made him stop talking, and that had my mother eyeing me with concern. "I've been a good son, I've always done as I've been told. But I'm not a little kid anymore. I'll be going to college next year and it's time for me to make my own choices."

I saw him open his mouth but this wasn't an argument and if I didn't collapse soon I'd start to think about Collette. About how she'd walked away from me...

"I'm a good son, Dad. And honestly? I'm a pretty great guitar player." I picked up the case and started up the stairs. "If you want to be a good father, you can find out for yourself." I glanced back to see them both at the bottom of the stairs, staring up at me like I was a stranger.

"Come support me at an audition tomorrow," I said. "If you really care about me and my future, then show up. Show me that you care about the future I've picked even if it's not the sort of future you planned."

I walked away before they managed to come up with a response.

For the second time tonight, I'd put myself out there and I wasn't about to stick around to see if I'd get burnt again. My heart could only handle so much rejection in one night. And losing Collette?

That was as much heartache as I could take.

EIGHTEEN

COLLETTE

There was a pit in my stomach that I couldn't get rid of. It felt like I'd swallowed a whole gallon of cement; it hardened inside of my body and wouldn't let go.

I'd felt so free and weightless while dancing with Ethan, but now it was as if I were wearing weights on my ankles and a cage around my soul. I couldn't shake this feeling that I'd lost some part of myself when I'd walked away from Ethan last night.

I wasn't me when I wasn't dancing and I wasn't me when I wasn't with Ethan.

It hadn't even been twenty-four hours since I'd seen or talked to Ethan but it felt like an eternity had passed. And when I'd see him again? Well, that was anyone's guess.

I overheard Mom talking to Coach Reynolds this morning as I got ready to leave. Apparently Ethan's dad had complained for the umpteenth time so he was releasing Ethan from his punishment. When the mayor wanted something, people bent over backwards to give it to him.

I tried to feel grateful that I wouldn't have to see Ethan

anymore. Not seeing him meant I would get over him that much faster. I wouldn't have to worry about him intruding in my life anymore.

I could finally collapse inside of myself like a dying star.

I shook off that sad thought. Not seeing him again was a step in the right direction. I'd move on. My life would go back to normal. I'd get over him...eventually.

But no amount of self-talk about why it was a good thing that Ethan was no longer part of my life seemed to help. Knowing that we were done just made the day drag on. Seconds felt like minutes and I wasn't sure if I could continue living my life in slow motion like this. If this was my new normal, kill me now.

"Psst."

I glanced over my shoulder to see Olivia offering me a soft smile. She mouthed *Are you okay?* And I just shrugged and turned back to my lab I was working on. Well, 'working on' was a stretch. I was doodling in the corner. I couldn't concentrate to save my life.

But I tried my best to keep my head down, to focus on my meaningless scribbles so I wouldn't have to pay attention to the dancers who'd been leaving class for their auditions.

Knowing the auditions were currently underway was a special form of torture. Wondering if Ethan was there—if he was really going to go through with it with or without me? That was killing me.

Out of the corner of my eye, I saw Olivia stand. I didn't think too much of it until suddenly, ice cold water was dumped down my back.

I yelped and shimmied out of my seat. I glanced up to see Olivia's surprised face. Her eyes were wide and her mouth shaped like an O.

"Oh my gosh, Collette, I'm so sorry," Olivia said as she

reached out to offer me assistance. I just glared at her. I loved my friend but being soaked and heartbroken had to be a new low for me.

Why stop digging at six feet when you could go to ten?

"What's going on here?" Mr. Baker asked as he hurried from his desk over to where we were standing.

"She...I'm..." Heat permeated my cheeks as I glanced around and saw the entire class staring at us.

I just waved to my now soaked shirt and marched out of the classroom. After all, Olivia did this to me, she might as well explain herself.

Just as the classroom door closed shut behind me, I heard Olivia say, "...I should make sure she's okay..."

Not wanting to wait for Olivia to start in on a round of, 'what's wrong' and 'why aren't you okay,' I hurried to the bathroom. Thankfully, I had a tank on underneath and as soon as I was at the hand dryer, I slipped off my shirt and stuck it under the air.

Olivia joined me a few seconds later. She kept talking but I couldn't hear over the roar of the dryer. I shook my head and shrugged as I watched her lips move. Hoping she'd pick up on the message that I didn't want to talk. Not to her. Not to anyone.

I could make out some of the things she was saying. Something about Ethan and dancing, but I'd made my decision. There was no going back now.

Suddenly, Olivia yanked my shirt from my hands and stepped back. There was a fire in her gaze that I'd never seen before. I scrambled to get it back from her, heat pricking at my neck.

What was the matter with her? Couldn't she see that I just wanted to be left alone?

The noise from the dryer stopped and an eerie silence

engulfed the room. I lunged for Olivia only to have her step to the side and raise my shirt over her head.

"Give it back," I said as I stood there with my hands on my hips, trying to give her the most menacing stare I could muster.

When she met my gaze, I wanted to cry. Olivia didn't seem angry or upset. Instead, she looked worried. That was so much worse. I could handle her anger right now. In fact, I craved it. Part of me wanted to yell and shout and slam my fists against the wall. But seeing her concern? Or worse...pity?

That I couldn't handle.

Olivia sighed. "I'm sorry I had to resort to such drastic measures, but you are shutting me out," she said as she shook out my shirt and grabbed a few paper towels and began blotting it.

I stared at her as I tried to process what she was saying. "You did this on *purpose?*"

Exhaustion swept over me and I leaned my shoulder against the wall as I watched her work.

Olivia snorted. "I'm a dancer. I have incredible balance." She smiled at me but then her expression morphed into one of concern. "You didn't answer my texts and this morning, I waited around for you in the courtyard but you never came." Her voice dropped to a hurt whisper. "We always meet in the courtyard."

Perfect. Now I could add 'being a crappy friend' to the list of why I sucked as a human. I swallowed, the cement from my stomach moving up to lodge itself in my throat. Tears stung my eyes and I shifted my body away from Olivia so she couldn't see them spill.

"Why won't you tell me what's going on?" Olivia's voice was closer and I glanced down at the ground to see she was standing right next to me.

I parted my lips, hoping something witty would come out, but nothing but a sob escaped.

I was a horrible human being. I wanted to dance. I wanted Ethan. I wanted my mother to be proud of me. I wanted the school to thrive. I wanted to pursue my dreams but I wasn't a glutton for punishment and I had no desire to live in a world filled with rejection and humiliation. I wanted to be a professional dancer and I wanted to not want to dance and I wanted Ethan but I didn't want to want him and...ugh, I was a mess.

I felt like I was being pulled in so many different directions but no matter which way I choose, someone always ends up getting hurt.

If I chose dancing and Ethan, then it would break my mother's heart.

If I chose my mother, then Ethan would never look at me like he had last night. But then he'd eventually find someone else. And I'd move on too, just without Ethan and without dancing. And as for Juilliard and the auditions? Well, the dancing world never knew I existed so I doubted they would care if I disappeared.

Olivia wrapped her arms around me and let me sob into her shoulder. All the worries. All the stress that I'd been carrying around for days slipped out. I was broken and hurting. Trying to cover a wound that felt as if it would never heal was killing me inside.

If I was ever going to become whole again, I needed to mourn.

And that's what I did. I mourned my future with Ethan and my future as a dancer.

Thankfully, I didn't cry forever even though it felt like I could. A few minutes later, my tears began to dry up and I stepped away from Olivia and into a stall where I grabbed a handful of toilet paper.

Once I was down to just sniffles, I turned and faced Olivia. I forced a smile and shrugged. "Thanks," I said.

Olivia nodded as she continued to blot at my shirt. Then she sighed as she tossed it to the side. "I've got a sweatshirt in my locker you can borrow. Now, are you going to tell me what's wrong or do I need to spill water on your pants as well?"

I raised my eyebrows as I studied her. From the tilt of her chin and her narrowed eyes, I knew she meant business. So I swallowed and walked over to the mirror where I began dabbing at my face. I looked like a mess, which was perfect.

I was a mess.

I sighed as I ran my hands under the water in front of me. There was something soothing about the shock that came from ice cold water touching your skin. It was waking me up which was nice. I was tired of living in a haze.

"I've given up dancing and Ethan," I mumbled as I watched the water trickle through my fingers.

"I'm sorry, what? Why?"

I inhaled slowly and then held my breath for a moment. Then I exhaled. I needed to remind myself why leaving everything I loved behind made sense. That this was what I wanted —no *needed*.

I glanced over my shoulder and shot Olivia a *please let this go* look. "It's the right thing to do." I pulled my hands from the water and shook the excess from my skin.

Olivia's expression didn't shift to one of understanding. Instead, the crease between her eyebrows deepened and she glared at me. *Glared* at me.

"You are ridiculous," she said as she folded her arms and met my gaze head on.

I parted my lips as I stared at her. "I'm sorry, what?"

She motioned to my body. "You are one of the most talented dancers in the entire school. You have as much potential in your one pirouette than I do in my entire body. You're beautiful and an incredibly handsome guy wants you." She sighed as she shoved her hands into the front pockets of her jeans. "I've seen the way he looks at you. He loves you. He adores you. And he wants you, just the way you are."

I parted my lips but I couldn't seem to find the words to speak. And then, reality hit me and tears sprung up again. I knew all of these things. I did. But they weren't the reasons I was walking away.

"The school is in trouble, Livi," I said as I turned. I hated that I was spilling this to her when it was Mom's secret, but I was tired of holding it inside.

"What?"

"The school. It's in trouble. If the scout doesn't pick someone from here, then the donors will leave and then this"—I waved my hands around the bathroom—"will be over."

I rested my hands on the sink in front of me and tipped my face down. I swallowed as my final words rang in the air.

When Olivia didn't say anything, I glanced over at her to see her frustration etched on her face. She was still mad at me? Why?

"That is the most ridiculous thing I've ever heard. You dumped Ethan and quit dance because you're trying to save the school?" She growled as she threw her hands up in the air. "You're not a savior, Collette. If this school is doomed to close, it has nothing to do with you. Quitting everything you love isn't going to save your mom or the students here." She stepped forward as she held my gaze. "It will only make you unhappy and full of regret."

I studied her as I let her words sink in. She was right. I knew she was right. My auditioning wouldn't hurt Bianca or Eve's chances of being picked. I wouldn't help save the school but my auditioning wouldn't hurt it either.

But it would save me from seeing my mother's embarrassment. It would spare me the pain of her disgust when she watched me dance.

I sucked in a deep breath as the truth of it landed like a punch in the gut.

Olivia was right. I was no savior...I was just scared. Scared of being rejected again and terrified of making a fool of myself.

And Ethan? Who did I think I would help by hurting the guy who'd done nothing but support me and my dreams?

Walking away from Ethan certainly wouldn't save the school. I shut my eyes tightly against the image of his pain as I'd told him no. As I'd turned away from him and his offer.

My gut churned as an ugly truth I didn't want to face started to surface. Walking away from Ethan had been hard, but it had been easier than facing his rejection. And deep down that was what I knew would come of being with him. One day he'd wake up and realize that I wasn't amazing. He'd finally lose those rose-colored glasses and see me as I really was, flaws and all. And when he did...would he still want me?

Olivia pulled me into a hug and then stepped back. "I know you, Collette. I know why you're pulling away. You're worried that who you are isn't good enough." She smiled at me and shrugged. "But you *are*. Everyone sees it but you."

I met her gaze and let myself hear her words. For the first time I forced myself to consider that maybe she wasn't just being nice because I was her friend. In fact, the more I thought about it, the more I realized that Olivia was never nice just to be nice, not even to me.

Olivia was honest. Brutally honest, in fact.

She placed her hands on my shoulders like she was my coach preparing to lay into me with some hard truths. "It's time you stop running away from what you want, Collette. It's time to start chasing your dreams."

I took a deep breath because what she was saying? It was terrifying. It was so frightening...because it was true.

"I don't know how to do that," I said.

Her eyes grew warm with sympathy. "Maybe you could start by trusting me when I tell you that you're more than enough—for Juilliard, for this school...for Ethan."

My heart did a weird little backflip at the mention of Ethan.

Olivia sighed. "Maybe you could start by trusting Ethan."

I let out a shaky breath as her meaning hit home. It was so hard to let myself believe that he might mean what he said. It was so much easier to listen to that voice that said he was mistaken, or he was blind, or he would change his mind. But why?

Why couldn't I choose to believe in Ethan rather than in that stupid voice that had been making me miserable for years?

Olivia squeezed my shoulders. "Be brave, Collette. Take a chance. Take the leap." She scrunched up her nose. "Now I sound like those motivational posters."

I laughed for the first time in a long time. And it felt amazing. As if I were releasing the pressure on the balloon that was my stress. So I laughed some more until tears filled my eyes.

Olivia stared at me with her eyebrows raised. I could tell she was confused but I couldn't stop so just waved my hand in her direction as I bent over and held my stomach.

She was right. On so many levels. And it was comical how wrong I'd been. How completely lame I'd been. I was the fool. I was the idiot who thought giving my life jacket to this school was the way to save it.

It wasn't.

"I'm so sorry," I said through the burst of laughter.

Olivia nodded but she still looked confused.

Thankfully, she stayed with me until I finished. I wiped my

cheeks as my expression grew serious. "You're right, Livi. I'm so sorry. I've been a lame friend." I furrowed my brow. "Can you forgive me?"

She stared at me for a moment before she slowly began to nod. "I think I can manage that."

I grabbed my shirt and pulled it on. It wasn't soaking wet which was good enough for me. Then I threaded my arm through Olivia's as we walked out of the bathroom. I swallowed as I tried to push down the fear that had crept up inside of me at the words I wanted to speak.

If I was going to be brave. If I was going to prove to Olivia and Ethan that I was the person they thought I was, then I needed to act.

I needed to put my money where my mouth was.

"So, do you think you can help me?" I asked suddenly, forcing the words out on an exhale.

Olivia glanced down at me. "With what?"

My whole body felt as if it were on fire, but I couldn't back down now. I was strong. I was a dancer. I could do this.

"Help me with the audition?"

NINETEEN

ETHAN

She wasn't coming.

I knew she wasn't coming, but that didn't stop me from craning my neck for a better view of the door.

She wasn't there, and I was left the idiot who thought our love could conquer her fears. That somehow, my feelings for her were all she needed to find her confidence.

Someone slap me now and wake me from my horribly optimistic nightmare.

The academy had assigned one of the smaller studios as a waiting room for all those who were auditioning. Dancers filed in and out, their expressions tense and their eyes not meeting mine as they stretched and warmed up. The anticipation in this room was nerve wracking. I had to remind myself over and over again that this audition wasn't that big of a deal for me. Juilliard wasn't even my dream.

It was Collette's.

I looked over to the door for the millionth time, trying to ignore the stab of bitter disappointment that flared up again. This audition couldn't end soon enough.

Part of me wanted to go out into the hallway to look for Collette, but the hall was filled with family members and teachers who were slipping in and out of the auditorium to watch the auditions.

I glanced over at Bianca and tried to focus on watching her warmup routine. It was better than sitting here in the corner like a chump, tuning my guitar for the twentieth time.

Bianca looked perfect. I mean, despite the classes, I still didn't know much about ballet. But she looked the part. All rigid lines and mind-blowing balance. But in my eyes she paled in comparison to Collette.

Of course, my opinion mattered to no one. Certainly not to Juilliard. But I couldn't help but note that while Bianca looked perfect—she had none of Collette's passion. Her expression was hard. Determined. She didn't get that dreamy look that Collette got whenever she danced.

She looked... Well, she looked kind of miserable.

Nothing at all like Collette.

"Dude, don't tell me you have a thing for the ice queen now." Ryan's voice jarred me out of my daze and I turned to see him sliding down the mirrored wall beside me so he was sitting next to me with his legs sprawled out.

He seemed comically laid back compared to the nervous, high-strung dancers in this room and it took me a moment of staring at him before I fully registered that he was *here*. At the academy. On a Friday morning. When he should have been at school.

"Ryan, what are you doing here?"

He gave me a lopsided grin. "What do you mean 'what am I doing here?' My best friend is about to audition for Juilliard. Did you really think I wouldn't come here to cheer you on?"

I shrugged. I hadn't really given it much thought either way. I'd told him about the auditions yesterday—I'd told him my plan. But I'd also told him that the only reason I was doing this was for Collette. "She's not going to show," I said. I kind of hoped that by saying it aloud, the idea would finally sink in. Like maybe if I openly acknowledged it, I'd stop waiting. I'd stop *hoping*. I'd stop looking at the door like some pathetic puppy dog.

His expression was sympathetic but he didn't try to argue the point. Which was good. I didn't want anyone to give me false hope and that's all it would be.

"Her loss, man," Ryan said.

I swallowed hard. That thought didn't make me feel better. It only made my heart ache on Collette's behalf. It would be her loss. She was the one who'd be missing out on a chance to go after her dreams. She'd be the one choosing to live with her insecurities and fears rather than take a leap of faith.

It would be her choice to go back to her old life of dancing alone, after dark...without me.

I let my head fall back against the mirror with a thud.

Nope, knowing that it was her loss definitely didn't make me feel any better. Her loss was my loss. And if she didn't show today, I'd be losing her for good.

"I don't know if I can do this, man." I said it quietly and for the first time in maybe forever Ryan didn't have a snarky comeback or even a lazy smile. He was one hundred percent serious when he turned to me.

"You're already doing it." He shrugged. "You showed up. That's all anyone can ask. You showed up for me and the band last night and you're showing up for your girl today." He nudged my arm with his elbow. "I'm proud of you, man."

The silence that followed was awkward. Ryan and I weren't big on emotional moments, and I had no idea how to tell him that his words meant a lot.

Ryan cleared his throat loudly. Way too loudly. Loudly enough that a certain prissy blonde took notice.

Bianca stopped mid-dancing to glare over at him. "What are *you* doing here?"

Ryan leaned closer to me. "Ten bucks says I can get the ice queen to smile," he said, his cocky smile returning.

I moved to say something, but Ryan had already made his decision.

He gave Bianca a smirk—one that always made her face redden and her glare to deepen during dance class. "I came to cheer you on, sweetheart," he said with a wink.

She narrowed her eyes in a frightening glare before turning her back on him and launching back into her routine as if he'd never interrupted.

Ryan leaned over with a loud stage whisper. "She loves me."

I shook my head with an exasperated huff of air—the closest thing to a laugh I could muster. "Yeah, you really have her wrapped around your finger."

He was grinning for real when he turned to me. "Hey, you might not have gotten the girl, but at least one good thing has come out of all this."

"Oh yeah? What's that?"

He nodded toward the door, which I'd been successful at avoiding since he sat down. "You finally stood up to your dad."

I whipped my head around to see...my dad? Shock had me staring with wide eyes as he entered the little studio, glancing left and right with a look of unease that spoke volumes about how out of place he felt.

Not surprisingly. I couldn't imagine my dad had spent much time at dance academies over the years.

My mother followed him in, looking stiff and stoic with her chin held high as she too took in the sight of all these girls. They spotted me before I could cover my surprise and in a few strides they were standing next to me as I scrambled to my feet.

Ryan nudged my arm again. "I'd better grab a spot in the audience. Make me proud, man."

He headed toward the door with a nod and smile for my parents and a 'break a leg, princess' for Bianca.

I was pretty sure I heard her snarl in return but I was too busy eyeing my parents. "What are you guys doing here?"

They exchanged a look as I held my breath. Sure, I'd been the ones to tell them about this audition and yeah, I'd invited them. But I hadn't actually thought they'd come. And now I had to wonder why they were here...was it to support me or to try and talk some sense into me?

My father cleared his throat. "Your mother and I have been talking..."

My mom gave me a little smile which eased some of the tension that had been building.

"We heard what you were saying," my father said, his voice so stiff it made him sound almost...nervous. "And we agree that perhaps you have a valid point."

My brows shot up in surprise.

"We've only ever wanted what was best for you," my mother said, her voice quiet and filled with a plea.

I nodded. "I know that."

Her smile was filled with gratitude, like she was worried I was going to yell at her or something.

"I understand you wanted the best for me," I continued, my own voice just as stiff as my father's because this was totally new territory for me. For us. My family never talked openly like this and doing it here, now...it was as awkward as it got. "But what you need to understand is that what's best for me might not always be what you envision."

My father's jaw was clenched tight and I waited for him to

start arguing. When he didn't, I pressed on. "What I need you to understand is that I want to make you proud. I do. But more than that I have to make myself proud."

I dipped my head to look down at the guitar. "I'm not sure yet what my future will hold, but I do know that I need the freedom to figure it out."

The silence that followed nearly crushed me with its weight.

When my father spoke I lifted my head to meet his gaze head on. "You're right." He cleared his throat again, a nervous tic I'd never seen before. "I raised you to be a leader, and that means making your own choices."

His jaw was still tight, his body too rigid. I could see what it took for him to say those words and relief swept over me, lightening some of the weight that had been crushing me. "Thanks," I said. "I appreciate that."

He looked away and then back to me. "I know I'm not always the best father, but I hope you know that I..." He cleared his throat. "That I love you."

He muttered it under his breath and quickly, like it was an embarrassing admission and that made me fight a laugh. "I know," I said. "And I love you too." I looked to my mom. "Both of you."

My father looked away again, shoving his hands in his pockets. "I'm not sure how to be the kind of father you deserve."

My heart clenched painfully in my chest at the raw admission. What Ryan said came back to me and I found myself repeating his words. "You showed up," I said. "That's a start."

He gave me a wan smile before nodding toward the door. "I guess we'll go find ourselves a seat, huh?"

I nodded. "Yeah, that would be...nice."

They walked away and I had one moment of peace before a

woman I didn't recognize walked in with a clipboard. "Ethan Morrison, you're up!"

"Good luck, Ethan." The normally quiet Eve shouted it from the other side of the room and I shot her a quick smile of gratitude as I headed toward the woman with the clipboard, guitar in hand...ready to make a fool of myself in front of my parents, Ryan, and a handful of Juilliard elite.

Awesome.

As the woman led me down the hall toward the auditorium, I cast one last look around for Collette, hating the disappointment that made me want to run out of here and never look back.

I couldn't do that because I'd made a promise. I'd told her I'd be here, that I'd play the guitar on this stage no matter what. I'd given my word and I'd see it through—I owed her that much.

After all, Collette had changed my life. She'd opened my eyes, she'd helped me see what I wanted, what made me happy, and how I'd been running away from it all like a coward. Whether she'd meant to or not, she'd helped me find the confidence I'd needed to stand up to my father.

Whether she'd meant to or not, she'd made me fall in love with her. And that wasn't something I could forget or walk away from...even if she could.

"You ready?" The lady with the clipboard looked frazzled and impatient.

"Ready as I'll ever be," I said.

She gave a short nod and threw open the door. I walked in to a silent, intimidating room with a small stage, a spotlight, and several rows of seats that were packed with people.

I couldn't make out all the faces thanks to the lights, and maybe that was for the best. If I was up there alone, I could pretend I was in the dance studio, playing only for myself and for Collette. I could ignore the questioning looks and the whispered questions of why a dance audition was being overrun by a mediocre guitarist playing Coldplay.

There were no seats on stage so I stood in the middle, holding my guitar up and looking one last time toward the door.

Nothing.

It was just me.

Alone.

"Whenever you're ready, Mr. Morrison," a voice called out.

I could have heard a pin drop in the silence of that auditorium. I gave a nod, unable to form words as I started to pluck out the first few notes of the song I knew by heart.

I'd only played two chords when my song was interrupted by the click of the door opening. My head snapped up, my hands froze.

I think I knew it was her before I even saw her. My heart knew the moment the door clicked. I saw her silhouette first, her perfect body a dark outline against the bright lights of the hallway.

And then she was moving toward me into the light, her expression filled with more emotions than I could read. Hope, fear, regret...love.

At least, I hoped it was love that had her eyes shining with unshed tears as she met my gaze and held it.

It might have been seconds or years—the silence between us was filled with meaning. Thankfully, my fingers took on a life of their own and music filled the air. It allowed me to stand there, completely consumed with my feelings of love and admiration for Collette.

My heart thudded painfully in my chest. Hope was overwhelming; it made my ribcage feel like it might burst with pressure, it made my pulse race and my heart leap.

It took everything in me not to drop the guitar and race toward her. I needed her in my arms more than I needed air to breathe.

But then she went up on tiptoe and I knew that was my cue.

She was doing this. My beautiful, graceful, passionate, perfect Collette was putting herself out there.

She was taking a leap of faith.

My heart nearly burst but I shoved aside my emotions and focused on my guitar. With a nod, I gave her the cue to start and we were off.

She was off. Dancing in the way that mesmerized me as my music filled the air. Her body light and graceful as she moved to the tune of Coldplay's *Fix You* the way she had so many times before.

But this time was different.

She was different.

And I had never been more in love.

TWENTY

COLLETTE

Never in my life had I ever gone from such a low to such a high in a matter of seconds. Every step I made toward the studio had my heart pumping and my chest feeling as if it would burst.

I had clung to Olivia, depending on her strength to guide me from the school section into the dance studio. And up until the point where we'd stood in front of the doors, I'd wanted to run. I'd wanted to leave and never look back.

But then I heard his music.

Ethan's music. It was faint and muffled, but I heard it. And all of my fear, everything that was keeping me from dancing—from being me—faded away.

There was nowhere else I wanted to be other than right here, dancing to his music.

I could feel his eyes on me as I leapt around the stage. He never took his gaze away from me as his fingers strummed the chords. The way he stood there, his concentration trained on me was both exhilarating and terrifying at the same time.

I knew he could see my flaws. I knew he was aware that I wasn't perfect. That I was never going to be perfect. And yet, I could feel his love for me in the way his lips tipped up into a smile. Or the way when he caught my eye, he winked in a sexy yet supportive way.

He had a way of taking all of my fears away. He saw in me something that I'd only begun to admit was even there.

He was my strength where I was weak.

Dancing to his music was something I was born to do.

I was fully and completely smitten with the man standing in the middle of the stage taking risks so that I could learn to be my better self. So I could be the person that he knew I was.

The final chords hung in the air as I extended out my leg and arm and held the final pose. I waited, the silence in the room deafening. I kept my gaze up, terrified that if I looked out to the crowd, I'd see the scouts' disgusted expressions.

Or worse, the disappointed look in my mother's gaze.

I wasn't sure how I was going to face her.

That was the cruel thing about dancing. While you're doing it, you're untouchable. Nothing in the world matters but the feel of the floor from your toes and the air around you as you leap through it.

But once the music stops. Once the movement ends...

Reality comes crashing down around you like a ton of bricks. And suddenly, you remember there is a world around you. Judging you.

And even though the thought of Juilliard, the school I'd dreamt about going to since the moment I rose up into my first relevé, was here, scrutinizing my body and my dancing, I was scared about what my mother thought.

"Thank you, you two. You can leave now."

I lowered my arms and stood there, taking a moment to bow. But before I even bent forward, Ethan appeared next to me and reached down to grab my hand. Warmth spread up my arm and exploded throughout my body as we bent forward to the roaring applause.

When we straightened, he didn't move to drop my hand—and I didn't make him.

I wanted the comfort that he gave if I was headed out of the studio to face my mother.

"You did amazing," he mumbled as he tipped his head toward me.

My cheeks flushed as I nodded. "Thanks. You too."

He squeezed my hand as he pushed open the door that led to the hallway. Once the door slammed behind us, we walked in silence, hand in hand.

The sound of a door opening broke the silence and my ears pricked as I slowed my gait. I didn't even have to look to know that it was my mother coming out of the audition room. And that she was headed straight for us.

"What was that about?" she asked.

My entire body stiffened as I fought the tears that threatened to spill. I knew I should turn around. I knew I should face my mother's disappointment, but I wasn't as strong as I thought I was.

I wasn't Ethan.

I clung to his hand as he stopped walking and from the corner of my eye, I saw him glance over his shoulder.

"Oh, hey, Ms. Boucher. Wasn't your daughter amazing?" He wrapped his arm around my shoulders and gently guided me to turn around.

I blinked a few times, trying to keep my tears at bay. I didn't want to care this much. I hated how I rested my value on what my mother thought. I wanted to be free of this pain that I'd been carrying around for too long.

"So this was your plan?" my mother said. "Asking for a

chance to audition so that you could sneak my daughter in front of the judges?"

Her words cut me to the core and I couldn't help but look up.

I expected to see the Ice Queen that I'd become accustomed to. I expected to see her hands on her hips and her gaze trained on me as she stared me down. I expected to see anger and resentment for going behind her back.

But I didn't see any of that.

Instead, her eyebrows were furrowed and her expression was soft as she ran her gaze over me. Her arms were folded across her chest as if she were trying to protect herself from something. Some truth that she couldn't quite face.

"You weren't going to let her," Ethan said. "And I'm sorry, Ms. Boucher, but your daughter was born to dance." I could hear the protective hint to Ethan's voice as his arm tightened around my shoulders.

Her gaze met mine and she looked...lost. "I thought you agreed that dancing wasn't in your future. You didn't fit in with the other girls. You don't have the right body type. I thought you didn't want to continue because you weren't cut out for it and..." She trailed off with a loud exhale. "You would have been hurt."

I knew what my mother was saying sounded mean, but she was confused. And hurting.

"I wanted to spare you from rejection," she said. I'd never once heard her sound so weak. So vulnerable. For the first time I saw her actions from her point of view—from the perspective of a woman who'd spent a lifetime being judged herself. Maybe she *had* been trying to protect me, in her own way. Maybe she'd never realized that her rejection was worse than anything I could face from my peers.

"I didn't want to see you hurt," she said quietly. "You'd experienced too much rejection already."

I pushed forward and wrapped my arms around my mother because I knew what she meant. My father's leaving us had been the worst kind of rejection. But he hadn't just left me... he'd left *us*. Tears streamed down my face as I held her. We'd never talked about Dad. We never shared emotions, but I was beginning to realize that it was the one thing we needed.

I needed my mom and my mom needed me.

"I'm sorry," I whispered as I pulled back.

For the first time since Dad walked out, my mother, Amiee Boucher, was crying as well. She reached up and held my face in her hands as she studied me.

"Nonsense, I should be saying sorry. I crushed your dreams. I tried to protect you from a world that you were obviously born to be a part of." She reached up and wiped my tears from my cheeks. "You were breathtaking. You were everything a dancer should be." She wrapped her arms around me and pulled me close again.

We held each other and cried. Everything we'd kept bottled up, all the words we'd never said to each other, were spoken in that hug.

"Can you forgive me?" she whispered.

I nodded. "Always."

She pulled away and then focused her attention on Ethan. She extended her hand and shot him a smile. "I have you to thank for the gift you've given me. You had faith in my daughter when I had none."

Ethan still looked confused but met my mom's gesture and shook her hand. "Well, she's incredible. Only a fool would keep her dancing in a studio by herself."

"Ethan," I said and shot him a look to which he just shrugged.

My mom held up her hand and shook her head. "Ethan's right. You are no longer dancing alone in a dark studio. I don't care what the Juilliard judges say, you will be dancing for the rest of your life."

My entire body flooded with excitement as I stared at my mom. "Really?"

She nodded as she reached forward and kissed both cheeks. "If you'll let me teach you, I would be honored to see where we can take your talent."

I threw my arms around her one more time. Then I pulled back and straightened my clothes. I knew my mom. When it came to dancing, she was all business. There was no place for emotions.

"Yes," I said. "I'd appreciate that."

Mom shot me a look that reminded me of why she was called the ice queen. Then she adjusted her bun, dabbed at her eyes, and then nodded to the both of us. "I need to go back in and finish these auditions." She walked by me but then paused as she glanced down. "We'll talk at dinner tonight?"

I smiled. "Yep."

She gave me a curt nod and then disappeared into the audition room.

Silence engulfed the hallway as I stood there, watching the door shut behind my mom. I felt as if I was living in some sort of alternative universe. Like I couldn't quite grasp the fact that all of my dreams were coming true.

Well...almost all of them.

There was one last one that I wasn't quite sure where we stood, but I was going to find out.

Suddenly, nervously, I began to pull at my shirt as I turned to face Ethan. His gaze was focused on his guitar as if he too felt as if he wasn't sure what to say.

I decided to get it out of the way and let my heart do the

talking. I leaned in and said, "Thanks."

His gaze snapped up to me and he held it for a moment before he shrugged. "Your mom is right. You're an incredible dancer. You deserve to be seen and the world deserves to see you dance."

I studied him, not able to fight the smile that emerged from his words. "And that's why I love you," I said. All of my emotions exploded through me at the same time causing my voice to drop to a whisper.

Ethan studied me and then turned. My heart plummeted as I watched him walk over to the wall. I knew I shouldn't have admitted something like that so soon. He was still hurt from my actions and I wouldn't blame him if he never forgave me.

But then, he set his guitar against the wall and turned back to face me. He walked toward me with an intensity that I'd never seen before. He looked determined and confident and my heart responded by galloping in my chest.

His hands were around my waist, pulling me close to him. I could feel his heart pound against my palms as my hands sprawled across his chest.

"I love you, Collette Boucher. You are the sexiest, sweetest, and most confusing girl I've ever been around." He tipped his forehead forward and rested it against mine. "But I can't stop thinking about you and I doubt I could ever stay away from you."

He dipped down and brushed his lips against mine.

Deep down, a dam broke inside of me and all the feelings of anger and hatred I had toward myself were washed away.

It was strange, seeing yourself through someone else's eyes. To Ethan, I was perfect. And to myself...I was beginning to accept that.

I didn't need to be who everyone thought I should be. I just needed to be me.

I slipped my hands from his chest up to the back of his neck where I threaded my fingers through his hair and pulled him closer, deepening the kiss.

Ethan must have taken that as my acceptance because his arms tightened around my waist and suddenly I was airborne. He spun me around and I broke our kiss for a moment so I could tip my head back and laugh.

I'd never felt so free. So...me.

He slowed down and set me back down on the ground. His arms remained wrapped around me and I didn't mind. I never wanted him to let me go.

His expression softened as he leaned forward and kissed my lips again. "You were amazing and if the Juilliard people can't see it, then they are blind."

I nodded as I leaned forward and rested my cheek on his chest. I could hear his heartbeat. It matched the rhythm of my own.

"It's okay," I said. And I really meant it. There was so much more to dancing than just getting into a prestigious conservatory. There were other schools and dance companies that did amazing things with ballet that the stuffy traditional schools would never accept. The dance world was always changing and evolving, and I would find my place within it. If it didn't exist already, I'd make a place for myself. I'd forge my own path.

Ethan just held me and we stood there, wrapped in each other's arms. Sure, we had no idea what the future was going to bring us. He still had Yale to figure out and I had a new relationship to build with my mother.

But it didn't matter. The fear was no longer coating my entire existence.

With Ethan by my side, I could conquer anything. And for the first time, I was realizing that I was the only one stopping what I could do.

If I wanted to dance, I had to put myself out there and do it.

And that thought excited me. More than anything had in a long time.

A wail pulled us apart as we glanced down the hallway. The audition door flung open and Ryan appeared, carrying a distraught Bianca.

She was gripping her leg and cursing. She glared at anyone who was trying to help—especially Ryan.

"You were a liability," she shrieked as tears streamed down her cheeks. "I told Ms. Boucher to keep you away from me and I was right. Look what you did."

Ethan and I pushed ourselves against the wall as the crowd that surrounded them hurried down the hall and out the doors of the school.

I turned to face Ethan whose eyes were wide and his surprised expression matched my own. He wrapped his arm around my waist and pulled me close to him. I snuggled in. I took a deep breath and rested my head on his chest.

"Don't you want to go see if she's okay?" he murmured.

I spread my hand out across his chest, reveling in the feeling of his voice as it reverberated through his ribcage. I shrugged and tipped my head back. "Nah. I think Ryan has it under control. Besides, I'd rather be here, with you."

Ethan kissed me again. This time longer and harder than he ever had before. It was as if he wanted me to know that he was never going to go anywhere. Like he wanted to show me how he felt.

And I lost myself in it. He was the one person who understood me and challenged me like I needed to be challenged.

I wasn't sure what our future held but I did know one thing, Ethan was going to be a part of it.

No matter what.

EPILOGUE

Ethan

Five Months Later

I GOT IN.

I still couldn't quite believe it, but the Yale acceptance letter was right there, sitting in front of me on the kitchen counter as proof.

"Are you going to sit here and stare at that piece of paper all night or are you going to help me and your sister set the table?" Collette's teasing voice asked as she nudged my shoulder, making me grin.

"Sorry," I said, folding up the paper. "I'm still trying to wrap my head around the fact that it's over."

She arched her brows in question as she handed over a stack of forks and knives for me to place on the napkins Chrissy had laid out. "What's over?"

"All these years of working my butt off," I said with a shake of my head. "It was all for this." I nodded toward the folded up letter and from the corner of my eye, I saw my parents come into the room.

Collette came over and slipped her arm through mine, her big eyes looking up at me in concern. "Are you disappointed?" she asked. "Is it anticlimactic or something?"

I shook my head slowly. "No, that's not it. I'm excited, I really am, it's just..." I shrugged as I struggled to find the right words. "I guess I just don't know what comes next."

Her smile was sudden and bright, and even after five months of dating and being joined at the hip, that smile still took my breath away. "Join the club," she said with a laugh.

I kissed the top of her head as I wrapped an arm around her, ignoring Chrissy's groans of disgust at the PDA. "I'm so proud of you, you know that, right?"

Collette squeezed my waist in return. "I know." She took a deep breath and let it out slowly. "And I should probably tell you that...I got in, too."

I backed up so I could stare at her in amazement, joy lighting up those beautiful eyes of hers. "You got into the Boston Conservatory at Berklee?"

She nodded quickly, her smile so big it lit up the room. I whooped with excitement and pulled her into my arms for a tight hug. "You are amazing," I said.

I could feel her smile against my neck as she squeezed me back. "Thanks. And I owe it all to you. I don't know if I ever would have had the nerve—"

"Yes," I interrupted. "You would have."

She sighed happily as we held each other tight.

I wouldn't lie and say everything had been super easy after the day of the auditions. One act of bravery didn't solve all of our problems. But it was the start of a new era for both of us.

Collette didn't get picked for the Juilliard role, but she and her mom did forge a new understanding. I think both Collette and her mom needed to get a little perspective, and that day they talked to one of the recruiters who gave them just that. The recruiter was impressed with Collette's talent and encouraged her to pursue dance, but to keep her options open.

Collette and her mom had spent so much time immersed in the world of ballet, with its strict rules and traditions, that they'd lost sight of everything else that was out there in the dance world. The recruiter helped them to see that it wasn't Juilliard or nothing. That it wasn't even ballet or nothing. There were other schools, other forms of dance, and other ways of pursuing the dream to dance on a stage.

And now my girl had gotten accepted into an amazing dance school, and I couldn't possibly be prouder.

She pulled back to look up at me. "Berklee is about two hours away, but I figure—"

"We'll make it work," I interrupted. "We always do."

She beamed up at me, because it was the truth. It wasn't always easy to make our relationship work between her dance training and my football, both of us had grades to keep up, and family relationships that were in dire need of attention...

But we made it work, because we loved each other. And that was something neither of us would ever take for granted.

"All hail the conquering hero!" My dad's booming voice filled the room as he and my mom walked over to join us.

I rolled my eyes behind my dad's back, making Collette and Chrissy giggle. Things with my parents have been...better. Our family was a work in progress just like Collette's relationship with her mom.

Their coming to watch me play guitar had been a step in the right direction, for sure. And they'd even been generous with their praise after the performance.

I think it still hurt their feelings that I'd been practicing in secret for all these years. I don't think they loved realizing how far we'd grown apart. But...things have slowly but surely gotten easier at home.

My dad didn't have a personality transformation overnight, but he's made efforts to ask my opinion first before shouting out commands about how I run my life. He's stopped giving me grief about going to ballet practices with the rest of the team. And my mom and dad both really like Collette so they've been supportive of me spending my precious free time with her.

"Dinner looks great, honey," my dad said. "The perfect meal to celebrate Ethan's acceptance into Yale."

Chrissy and I exchanged a funny little grimace. That was another change around here. My parents had started couples' therapy and they were now being so nice to each other it was kind of cringe-worthy.

But good for them, right? If it meant that Chrissy would be in a less toxic household next year when I was off at college, I was all for it.

I held out a seat for Collette before sliding into my spot beside her. "Collette has good news, too—" I started, but Collette cut me off with an elbow in the rib and quick shake of her head.

"Tonight's your night," she said quietly so only I could hear. "We'll celebrate me another time, but for tonight...let's just enjoy the fact that you worked hard and it paid off."

I squeezed her hand under the table. "I love you, Collette."

"I love you, too." She leaned over to give me a peck on the cheek as my mom started dishing out food.

"To Yale's newest student," my dad said as he lifted his glass for a toast.

The rest of us lifted ours as well and Collette touched her glass to mine. "You know, I think you were wrong before when you said it's over." She grinned when I met her gaze. "Our next adventure is just about to begin."

***

We hope you enjoyed Collette and Ethan's story! We had a blast writing it and can't wait to share Ryan and Bianca's story next. Turn the page for a bonus chapter to see how their story begins!

Head on over to Amazon and grab your copy TODAY!

The Running Back and the Prima Donna
Book 2 of the Ballet Academy Series
HERE
He thought he had her figured out.
He was wrong.

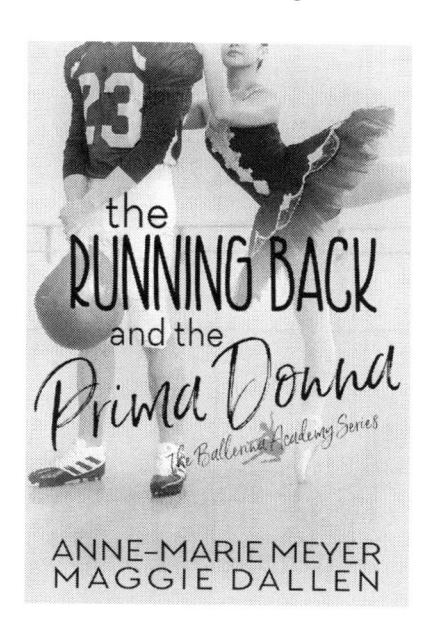

***

About the Authors

Maggie Dallen is a big city girl living in Montana. She writes adult and young adult romantic comedies in a range of genres. An unapologetic addict of all things romance, she loves to connect with fellow avid readers on Facebook, Twitter or at www.maggiedallen.com.

To keep up to date with her new releases (and for giveaways, sale alerts, and sneak peeks), sign up for her monthly newsletter at http://eepurl.com/bFEVsL

Or visit her Amazon page for more fabulous reads! https://www.amazon.com/Maggie-Dallen/e/B01914ZJIS

Anne-Marie Meyer lives south of the Twin Cities in MN. She spends her days with her knight in shining armor, four princes, and a baby princess.

When she's not running after her kids, she's dreaming up romantic stories. She loves to take her favorite moments in the books and movies she loves and tries to figure out a way to make them new and fresh.

Join her newsletter at https://BookHip.com/HZXKNT or connect with her on Facebook or Instagram or her website www.anne-mariemeyer.com

Or visit her Amazon page for more fabulous reads! https://www.amazon.com/Anne-Marie-Meyer/e/B074X7RJGF

BONUS CHAPTER

Bianca

At the auditions...

"BIANCA JONES AND EVE LAWSON, you're up next."

I nodded to the woman with the clipboard as those dumb butterflies took flight in my stomach. She was one of the Juilliard judges and it wouldn't do to let her see my nerves. Let the rest of these clowns be unprofessional; I would be the epitome of calm, cool, and collected.

Fake it 'til you make it. That was one of the first life lessons I'd ever learned and it had always served me well. None of the other students here seemed to get that. They were so quick to show their hand, to whisper and giggle with one another about how excited they were or how nervous they felt.

Amateurs, the lot of them.

"Bianca," Eve prompted, as if I hadn't heard. I'd heard, I just refused to rush. I wasn't a dog who came when someone whistled. I was a professional, which in this world meant one thing—I was a prima ballerina.

Or at least, I would be.

The lady with the clipboard was watching me with obvious impatience and I gave her my most ingratiating smile. "Coming," I said as I shrugged off the sweatshirt that had been keeping my muscles warm and loose.

The clipboard lady softened at the smile. They all did. Smiles, like words, were weapons to be wielded, and I'd figured out a long time ago that if you used them sparingly and wisely, smiles could be effective.

I knew what all the other dancers said about me. They thought I was cold, heartless...maybe I was. But I knew what they didn't.

Nice got you nowhere.

Confidence was key.

But none of that meant anything without drive. The will to succeed. I followed the Juilliard rep with Eve prancing excitedly next to me. "Can you believe it?" she whispered. "Juilliard."

Her voice was filled with awe and reverence.

I ignored her. I didn't have time for chitchat. I needed every ounce of my attention and focus centered on one thing.

My audition.

This was it. The moment I'd been training for my entire life.

"Are your parents in the audience?" Eve continued. "Mine are."

I shot her a sidelong glare that I hoped would shut her up. I usually didn't mind Eve. But then again, she was usually quiet.

Apparently nerves made her chatty.

Lucky me.

"Did they come to cheer you on?" Eve continued.

I let out a loud exasperated sigh of impatience. Had my parents come? Of course not. They didn't believe in coddling, and I didn't need hand holding. I worked better when I was alone, and my family knew that.

"Mine are watching," Eve said.

"How nice for you," I said in a monotone voice that expressed clearly just how little I cared about Eve or her family. And why should I? Eve, like every other girl in this school, was competition. End of story.

"Bianca, you'll go first," the assistant said as she held open the door to the auditorium. "Eve, you'll wait here with me."

"Break a leg," Eve hissed as I walked into the room.

I kept my eyes on center stage, not giving in to the temptation to look at the scouts or the parents and friends who weren't here for me. Most of these people were hoping I'd fail. If I did, then maybe one of their darling daughters would win the coveted spot.

I tilted my chin up high as I climbed the short flight of stairs and headed into the spotlight.

I focused on those haters, on their ill-will. Competitiveness was a better way to focus my energy than being nervous or worrying about what the recruiters saw when they watched me go into my opening stance.

The lights were blinding me as the first strains of music came from the speaker. My inner metronome turned on as I counted out the beats, readying myself for the routine that I could now do in my sleep.

One, and two, and three, and start...

A ballerina in a music box—that was what my first teacher had compared me to back when I'd first started. She'd meant it as a compliment and it was what I envisioned every time I danced. A beautiful, porcelain figurine moving with precise movements in perfect synchronicity with the music.

One, and two, and three...

Perfection. My movements were perfection. I knew it. I could feel it. All the intensive training these last few weeks had been worth it because my movements were effortless and graceful and—

Pop! My ankle seemed to tear in two. Pain scorched through my leg and I lost my balance. I swallowed a scream of agony just before it left my lips, but it was too late to recover the moment.

I fumbled with the next step as sweat broke out along my forehead and all the blood seemed to rush from my head to my feet.

No, this could not be happening.

Through the music I heard voices, murmurs of concern as I tried to resume where I'd left off.

My stupid ankle wouldn't let me. The pain was unbearable whenever I placed weight on it.

No! Not now. This could not be happening.

Air was coming in short gasps as I tried to breathe through the pain. I couldn't get enough oxygen, but I was so close to the finish. If I could just make it through—

Someone leapt onto the stage.

What the... Was that...

"Ryan?" His name came out on a rush of air as shock made me still. I couldn't even pretend to continue dancing when Ryan stalked toward me. His normal smirk was gone. His brow was furrowed in concern as he strode across the stage.

"What are you doing?" I asked.

He leaned down. "Come on, princess, let's get you out of here."

"No," I said through gritted teeth. I was horrified to

discover tears were streaking down my cheeks. I swiped at them and then turned on him, smacking his chest as he wrapped his arms around me and lifted me up.

"What do you think you're doing?" I demanded.

The pain was temporarily forgotten as he swept one arm under my knees so he was cradling me in his arms. "Stop it," I screeched.

He didn't listen.

"I can't stop," I said. Even I could hear the panic in my voice, but honestly...he was ruining everything. "Put me down right now."

"You're hurt," he said.

He looked down at me and for a second I forgot to breathe. For a heartbeat, I forgot my anger and panic and the pain that was making my whole leg throb. His eyes were so dark with emotion, so filled with concern...

For me.

No one had ever looked at me like that.

Then he started walking off stage and I finally came to my senses. "Put me down!" I was shrieking like a harpy but I didn't care. This was it. This was my moment. And he was ruining everything. "Put me down, you idiot. I have to finish."

He didn't respond until we were out of the auditorium and back in a studio that was dark and deserted. "It's over, Bianca."

I realized I was still smacking his shoulders, pounding on his back as he set me down gently on the floor.

His voice was quiet in my ear. "It's over."

"No." I shook my head, glaring up at him as he reached for his phone.

"You need a doctor," he said, ignoring my protest.

"I don't need a doctor, I need to finish my audition." That panicky feeling was back because...oh holy crap, what had he done? I reached out and shoved him as hard as I could you.

"You did this," I sobbed through my tears. "You ruined everything."

***

Head on over to Amazon and grab your copy TODAY!

The Running Back and the Prima Donna
Book 2 of the Ballet Academy Series
HERE
He thought he had her figured out.
He was wrong.

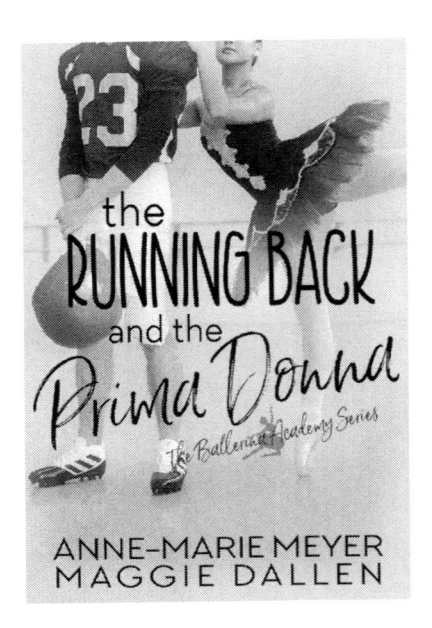